Handprints on My Heart

I love you Miff!

—Marian

**by the students in the
Rutherford County, Tennessee
School System**

Wax Family Printing, LLC
Murfreesboro, TN

Copyright © 2010 by
Rutherford County Tennessee School System
2240 Southpark Blvd.
Murfreesboro, TN 37128

All rights reserved.
Published by Wax Family Printing, LLC
www.waxfamilyprinting.com

ISBN 0-9815604-6-5 Paperback

Title: Handprints on My Heart, multiple authors.
Subject: Literary Collections, Poetry.

Project Sponsor:
Rutherford County Tennessee Board of Education
Harry Gill, Jr., Director of Schools

Project Coordinators:
Elizabeth Church, Language Arts Instructional Specialist
Jackie Drake, Administrative Assistant
Cover Design: Front Cover: Ana Kirkham, Siegel High School, Grade 12
Back Cover: Drew Stockham, Parker Roark,
    and Calli Beth Schlick, Brown's Chapel Preschool
Inside Cover: Marshall Morgan, Christiana Elementary School, Grade 5

For Wax Family Printing:
Publisher: Kevin Wax
Inside Layout: Angel Pardue

To publish a book for your school or non-profit organization that complements your academic goals or values, vision and mission, please contact:

Wax Family Printing, LLC
215 MTCS Drive
Murfreesboro, TN 37129

phone: 615-893-4290
fax: 615-893-4295
www.waxfamilyprinting.com

Table of Contents

Introduction/*Harry Gill, Jr.* ....*xiii*

Carrying the Torch/*Paul Kovacic* ....*xv*

Chapter One
Handprints of Family

Sibling Rivalry / *Elliott Todd* *3*
Marigolds and Asters / *Millie Harrison* *4*
One of a Kind Relationship / *Karson O'Bryan* *5*
My Grandfather Thomas / *Thomas Gray* *6*
I Am Hurt / *Sable Gilliland* *6*
My Father / *Abigail Woodson* *6*
My Sister / *Bryan Lopez* *7*
My Mom / *Krysta Forsberg* *7*
Family Trip / *Alexander Salvatore* *7*
Handprints on My Heart / *Jayen Patel* *7*
Son's Love / *Benjamin Bishop* *7*
Family / *Alyssa Bolton* *8*
Handprints on My Heart / *Kylie Tarver* *8*
What Makes My Heart Happy / *Zachary Stong* *8*
The Specialist Mom / *Alyssa Mealer* *8*
My Brother Drew / *Ashley Perhac* *9*
Memories of Granpa Vanek / *Jessie Kearney* *9*
Handprints / *Sivilay Nick Chanthaseng* *9*
Dear Dad / *Erika Easterly* *10*
When My Brother Came Along / *Gracie Range* *10*
The Letter I Can Never Send / *Mariah Smith* *11*
Handprint on My Heart / *Bekkah Riley* *11*
He Leaves a Handprint on My Heart / *Erika Dean* *12*
Handprint on My Heart / *Peri Watson* *13*
Artwork by A.J. Taylor *13*
You Left a Handprint on My Heart / *Rachel Smetana* *14*
Family / *Collin Gabel* *14*
Handprints on My Heart / *Diamond Morrison* *15*
My Family and Me / *Alyssa Watson* *15*
My Brother / *Gabe Martin* *15*
A Marine's Life / *Shelby Eberwein* *16*
Searching / *Amanda Ward* *17*
Handprints on My Heart / *Allison Howard* *18*

Little Kaiden Carter / *Christian Sims* *19*
My Granny Loved to Fish / *Spencer Hutchins* *19*
A Mother Like You / *Torryn Windrow* *20*
Grandma / *Isabelle Hydrick* *20*
For My Mommy / *Christina Wells* *21*
Parents / *Jessica Polsinelli* *21*
My Grandma / *Patrick Cardel* *22*
Handprint on My Heart / *Carrington Creasy* *22*
Grandma Ollie / *Maggie Harris* *23*
My Cousin / *Jevon Lee* *23*
Dear Ma / *Macey Sweeton* *23*
A Mother's Love / *Shelby Follis* *24*
My Dad / *Bain Smith* *24*
Dear Papa / *Taylor Robinson* *24*
My Parents / *Katherine Kimball* *25*
Lasagna / *Kennedy Blackwood* *25*
My Grandma / *Nicholas Mitchell* *25*
Bill / *Mia Cortner* *26*
Sandra / *Alexis Goodson* *26*
My Special Person / *Lexy Curry* *26*
Hand on My Heart / *Carson Farley* *27*
Role Model / *Alexandria Moore* *27*
What's Special to Me? / *Matthew Connors* *28*
I Remember / *Allison Hatfield* *28*
My Grandfather / *Ashley Harper* *29*
My Brother / *Dajiah Platt* *29*
Dad, Will You Please Come Home? / *Hailey Haraway* *30*
Our Little Tradition / *Maria Quaintance* *30*
Mom / *Brandon Ray* *31*
I Miss You / *Stephanie Davis* *31*
For the Mothers of the Class of 2010 / *Lauren Hendrix* *31*
One Choice Can Change a Life / *David Rice* *32*
A Mother's Love / *Austin Bradford* *32*
My Family in 2008 / *Tyler Stout* *33*
To My Grandma Who Changed My Life / *Karsen Daniel* *33*
Just My Daddy and Me / *Morgan Herring* *33*
A Handprint on My Heart / *Krista Martin* *34*
Handprints on My Heart / *Trevor Sharber* *35*
My Brother / *Logan Moore* *35*
My Unborn Niece / *Gracie Walden* *35*
My Other / *Kayla Stiles* *36*
A Place I Love / *Elizabeth Nelson* *36*
Move On / *David Najera* *36*
My Sister / *Sarah Merritt* *37*

My Family / *Austin Gamble* *37*
On My Dad's Birthday / *Ava Palmer* *37*
Grandpa / *Peyton Milam* *37*
My Inspiration / *Victoria Clowers* *38*
Big Mawmaw / *Grant York* *38*
My Dad / *Savanna Morrow* *39*
My Mom / *Caitlin Lister* *39*
My Family / *Hayden Rumpf* *40*
My Family / *Amber Hurt* *40*
Artwork by Christina Vongsiharath *40*
She Helps Me Fly / *Crystal Meadors* *41*
I Remember / *Yeilen Rodriquz* *42*
Eddie / *Kaley Humphrey* *42*
Her Knitting / *Tori Hawkins* *43*
Pap / *Molly Underwood* *44*
Why I Love U / *Nathan Price* *45*
My Brother / *Nicole Gardner* *46*
Her Survival Story / *Katie Stotler* *47*
One of a Million / *Erica Roberts* *48*
My Brother / *Steven Granados* *49*
My Love / *Achok Alier* *49*
Cancer Survivors / *Rebecca Lawless* *49*
My Brother Nick / *Wyatt Parkhurst* *50*
Iraq / *Kayla Forren* *50*
Mommy / *Asianna Vongvirath* *50*
My Family / *Tucker McAdoo* *50*
Parents / *Brooke Adams* *51*
Handprints on My Heart / *Lauryn Cole* *51*
Handprints on My Heart / *Taylor Murphy* *51*
Handprint on My Heart / *Abbey McAdams* *52*
Grandpa and Me / *Lane Herman* *52*
My Mom / *Katie Hagar* *52*
Older Sisters / *Victoria Wade* *53*
Because You're Gone / *Anais Lopez* *54*
I Miss You, Papa / *Kristin Bowers* *55*
My Grandma / *Rheannon Hart* *56*
Baby Sister / *Lily Springer* *56*
My Grandparents / *Jace Berry* *56*
Lee-Lee / *Kaleia Branch* *56*
Bizarre Family / *Kaleb Lewis* *57*
Handprints on My Heart / *Alexis Underwood* *58*
My Parents / *Marianna Ford* *58*
Artwork by Marianna Ford *58*
Handprints on My Heart / *Jailyn Hicks* *59*

Handprint on My Heart / *Jessica Patel* *59*
My Sister / *Diane Olvera* *60*
Artwork by Diane Olvera *60*

Chapter Two
I Am Handprints

Bug / *Layne Nash* *63*
From the Family / *Nicholas Ged* *64*
I Am From / *Hannah Adkins* *65*
I Am Who I Am / *Cameron Boupharath* *66*
I Am / *Leeah Crenshaw* *67*
I Am / *Autumn Kimble* *68*
I Am / *Tiffany Quigley* *68*
I Am / *Olivia Weaks* *69*
I Am / *Elim Jo* *69*
I Am / *Bailey Peacock* *70*
Alec / *Alec Berkstressor* *70*
Sydney / *Sydney Westergard* *71*
James / *Malachi Jones* *71*
I Am / *Christian Trabal* *71*
Mirrors / *Faith Matherly* *72*
MJ / *Emily Joiner* *72*
Bee / *Emily Nash* *73*
Buzz / *Cade Mills* *73*
I Am / *Eden Halverson* *74*
Why I'm Me / *Nash Binkley* *75*
That's Me / *Alexis Seilkop* *76*
I Am From / *Hunter Ozment* *77*
I Am From / *Kelsey Brown* *77*
I Am / *Edwin A. Rodriguez* *78*
Artwork by Steven Roberts *78*
Who I Am / *Kelsey Keith* *79*
I Am / *Jazmyn Carothers* *80*

Chapter Three
Handprints of Memories

I Remember / *Arisa Ozaki* *83*
Mississippi / *Cassady Compretta* *83*
Beauty Masked by Danger / *Katie Bentley* *84*

Handprints on My Heart / *Rumbi Tawoneui* 86
Never Let Go / *Kayleigh Snyder* 87
Artwork by Austin Lewis 87
Me and My Dad / *Mitchell McGuire* 88
Taking a Picture / *Jaden Layne* 88
The Ferocious Bull / *Miguel Bello* 89
My Trip to Disneyland / *Garrett Stirewalt* 89
Parents / *Alexis Laye* 89
Memories / *Lin Ni* 90
Memories / *Kristen Marr* 90
What Is a Special Time? / *Jackson Cole* 91
Saturday Morning / *Iris Saunders* 91
Cooking with My Great-Grandmother / *Maiah Case* 92
Christmas / *Sam Chappin* 92
Artwork by Bailey Hughes 92
I Remember / *Ellen Williams* 93
The Big Game / *Haylee Ferguson* 94
Home Sweet Home / *Savannah Berry* 95
Preschool Handprints / *Aleah Nicholson* 95
Football / *Logan Parker* 96
My Rabbits / *Jake Wiebe* 96
I Remember When / *Hannah Cron* 97
Dear Mom / *Kent Srisavanh* 97
The Contest / *Danielle Driver* 98
Footprints in the Sand / *Michaela Marcum* 100
Graveyard Hunting / *Emily Sellers* 101
Ode to Jeffery / *Kirstin Williams* 102
Going to Disney World / *Carson Boyd* 102
The Little Girl in the Big Woods / *Chloe Ownby* 103
Fall Fun / *Kendall Miller* 103
A Day at the Beach / *Jordan Watkins* 103
Nonnie's Camping Trip / *Riley Carter* 103
We Went to the Fair! / *Morgan Reasonover* 104
My Dog / *Devron Burks* 104
My Trip / *Savannah Bowen* 104
Swimming with the Wild / *Sydney Russom* 105
Memories / *Noelle Henson* 106
My Vibraphone / *Keaton Davis* 107
Reflections of Joy / *Amy St. John* 109
Artwork by Kylea Carver 109
Tara / *Emily Duchac* 110
The Once a Year Trip / *Jenny Newman* 111
The China Rabbit / *Natalie Palmer* 112
Just Like Me / *Caitlin Meier* 113

Christmastime / *Yuleni Cardenas* 113
When I Was Little / *Adam Close* 114
The Time I Went to Florida / *Kaylee Phifer* 114
How I Lost My First Tooth / *Shayla Mayo* 114
We Go Camping / *Michael Lahue* 115
First Day of High School / *Bailee Dover* 115
The Fight / *Vince Phillips* 116
I Did That / *E.J. Majors* 117
Fishing Poles / *Josh Carpenter* 117
Sport / *Anna Elizabeth Vogler* 118
Cheerleading / *Kyndall Brooks* 118
My Dog Black / *Kristin Demonbreun* 119
Christmas / *Kylea Carver* 120
My Level 6 Year / *Hannah Tomlinson* 120
Memories: Beautiful Scenes / *Robyn Sharp* 121

Chapter Four
Life's Handprints

Hope / *Brent Nevar* 125
Not Just a Handprint / *Siori Koerner* 125
Handprint on My Heart / *Rebecca Lopez* 126
Artwork by Jenny Peters 126
Safe Haven Family Shelter / *Meredith Mills* 127
The Heart's Canvas / *Caitlin Lee* 127
I Do Not Understand / *Daniel Graham* 128
Chasing / *Shelby Bolton* 128
Understand? / *Chianti Hill* 129
Handprint on My Heart / *Virginia Tipps* 129
Handprint on My Heart / *Mason Shadrick* 130
Loving Life / *Bryan Beyal* 130
Hope / *Esther Soper* 131
Three-Part Heart / *Kandace Clark* 131
Handprints on My Heart / *Collinthia House* 132
Rocky, the Great Horse! / *Abby Cerna* 132
The First Day of Second Grade / *Lauren Miller* 133
The Horrible Social Studies Paper! / *Katie Lang* 134
Best Friends / *Taryn Taylor* 135
What Love Is / *Jessica Farler* 135
To Have / *Brittney West* 136
Artwork by Katie Goins 136
The Turning of Hearts / *Austin Poteete* 137
Worrying / *Emyle Lawrence* 137

Shaken Waters, Still Land / *Sara Wylie Helton* *138*
Not All Things / *Andario Howard* *138*
Those People in Life / *Madison Baird* *139*
Friends / *Denis Korobkov* *140*
Are You Still Here? / *Alexandria Hunter* *140*
Will You Be There? / *Courtney Goodman* *141*
He Is / *Griffin Dodd* *142*
The Pet I Love / *Sydney Barnett* *142*
Artwork by Mollie Stone *142*
My Dream / *Emma Arnette* *143*
What Have I Become? / *Eli Ragland* *144*
Touched My Heart / *Mason Nolan* *144*
Dig Inside Your Heart / *Nathan Clark* *145*
This Way / *La'Shay Johnson-Clay* *145*
Friends Argue / *Taylor Canter* *146*
U.S.A. Heart to Heart and Hand to Hand / *Gabriel Pledger* *146*
Artwork by Karys Goostree *146*
America Is a Place / *Rachel Yates* *147*
Handprints on Heart Story / *Addison Gentry* *147*
Painful Memories / *Elizabeth Davenport* *148*
Autumn Falls / *Amisha Mitchell* *149*
Night / *Tanner Jones* *149*
Ode to Our Teacher / *Savannah Berry and Lindsay Randolph* *150*
Handprints / *Nicholas Emerton* *150*
The Pony / *Mollie McDonald* *151*
Impressions on My Life / *Kaneisha Jordan* *152*
Artwork by Lindsay Wick *153*
Sweet Dreams / *Katelyn Worley* *154*
Why? / *Ciera Powers* *154*
Christmas / *Kalyn Patterson* *155*
A Boy and a Poem / *Marty Council* *155*
Pasture Full / *Hunter Faulk* *156*
Flight / *Doug Brown* *156*
I Once Told a Friend / *Morgan Rhoades* *157*
Checkers / *Allie Davis* *157*
You Saved Me / *Alejandra Carrillo* *158*
Artwork by Heather Allen *158*
Target Practice / *Kaitlyn Whittle* *159*
Meant to Be / *Tabitha Smitty* *159*
My Game / *Katie Williams* *160*
The Perfect Words / *Brittany Maxwell* *160*
Change / *Reggie Pierre-Paul* *161*
Rock Friend / *Victoria Olds* *162*
First of Many / *Christopher Nobile* *163*

Look Beside You / *Chelsea Nicholson* *164*
My Dog / *Kelly Day* *164*
Home / *Ashley Colemon* *165*
Artwork by Parker Hewitt *165*
My Selfless Dream / *Bailey Carpenter* *166*
Lemon / *Brian Williams* *166*
The Christmas Miracle / *Shelby Jones* *167*
Best Friends Forever / *Hayden Petty* *168*
Quiggly / *Andy King* *168*
Basketball / *Mack Ferrell* *169*
Handprints on My Heart / *Chris Smith* *169*
Handprints on My Heart / *Cassidy Conard* *170*
Handprints on My Heart / *Kennedy Wallace* *170*
The Dream for Me / *Kristen Hunsicker* *171*
I Want to Be / *Sydney Henn* *172*
Handprints on My Heart / *Delaney Mitchell* *172*
Someone Like Me / *Sydney Dodd* *173*
Dream of a Better World / *Lindsay Bouldin* *173*
I Don't Know / *Grace Scruggs* *174*
One Chance / *Kane Wilkerson* *174*
Lily / *Alexia Halford* *174*
Labels / *Dominique Woodard* *175*
Fall / *Kailey Butler* *175*
School Is Fun / *Annabelle Diefenbaugh* *175*
Levi / *Ethan Day* *176*
My Hamster / *Shaylee Ezell* *176*
My Teacher / *Vivian Seay* *176*
Handprints on My Heart / *Claire Cahoon* *176*
Widgets / *Christine Choo* *177*
Identical / *Lauren Pearson* *177*
Who? / *Jacob Schultz* *178*
Touch Every Heart with Love / *Nausheen Qureshi* *178*
Flying / *Ellen Allbritten* *179*
Signs of Winter / *Megan Meadow* *179*
Simply Rain / *Brian Allen* *180*
Home Is Where the Heart Is / *Caroline Daws* *181*
Outside / *Graham Bateman* *181*
On a Cold Winter Day / *Savannah Lee* *182*
They Need Our Help / *Aran Moran* *182*
Fathers / *Christopher Haley* *183*
My Best Friend / *Ashley Gray* *183*
Feelings of My Heart / *Rodolfo Danny Martinez* *184*
I Wonder / *Adrian Garcia* *184*
My Best Friend / *Madison Nippers* *185*

My First Recital / *Kaylee Flores* *185*

Bugs / *Grace Scivicque* *185*

Happy Halloween / *Alyssa Rhinehart* *186*

Summer Makes Me Happy / *Dallen Garrett* *186*

My Cat Tigger / *Malayna Wacaster* *186*

Kindergarten / *Noah McAlister* *186*

Genuine Patriot / *Megan Taylor* *187*

A Storybook / *Peyton Fogle* *188*

Things That Make Me Happy / *Alexis Crank* *188*

Fall Leaves / *Katie King* *189*

Thank You / *Tionne Emmons* *189*

This Is What Makes Me Happy / *Samara Simmons* *190*

I Like To / *Collin Dye* *190*

Marines / *Caleb Lay* *190*

Sherman / *Ridge Sessions* *190*

Maggie / *Rachel Foster* *191*

My Hope for Soccer / *Samantha White* *191*

My Favorite Place / *Mattie Webb* *191*

Softball / *Hailey Lopez* *192*

Thanksgiving / *Kaitlyn Estes* *192*

My Pet Giraffe / *Faith Buck* *192*

A Boy's Journey to Fly / *Trevor Gaines* *193*

My Dog Duke / *Mallory Mosier* *194*

The Train Museum / *Josiah Fulk* *194*

Army Soldiers / *Taylor Gilpin* *195*

Fourth of July / *Allison Haeker* *195*

Thanksgiving / *Nathan Farrington* *196*

Thanksgiving / *Kendall Hughes* *196*

Art / *Caton Taylor* *196*

Christmas / *Ashlyn Hargrove* *197*

My Triathalon / *Tyler Nelson* *197*

Basketball / *Sabrea James* *198*

My Hopes and Dreams of Motorcross Mornings / *Bradley Carrithers* *199*

Life Lesson / *Bryan Daley* *199*

RUTHERFORD COUNTY BOARD OF EDUCATION

Harry Gill, Jr., Director of Schools

2240 Southpark Boulevard
Murfreesboro, Tennessee 37128
Phone (615) 893-5812   Fax (615) 898-7940

February 9, 2010

Dear Reader,

<u>Handprints on My Heart</u>, the eleventh book in a series of outstanding books published by the Rutherford County Board of Education, is a collection of writings and illustrations. The stories, poems, letters, and artwork reveal our students' most heartfelt thoughts and hopes, sharing the influences of their life journeys.

Each student's writing reveals a handprint of a time that shares special memories, dreams, or reflections on life. From Paul Kovacic's poignant memoir of his grandfather's hands, to the inspiration of hope found in Brent Novar's poem, to Bryan Daley's description of the lessons life teaches, I admire each student's strength and ability to see the goodness life holds.

As you read, I encourage you to look within your own heart, finding the precious handprints waiting there.

Best regards,

Harry Gill

Harry Gill, Jr.
Director of Schools

Moving Beyond Excellence

Carrying the Torch
Paul Kovacic
Siegel High School, Grade 12

As I walked by his open casket, I wondered how I would react. Would I burst into tears? Would I even be able to look at his body? It occurred to me that I was not even looking at a person, but a memory of a person. A pesky fly whizzed by me, oblivious to the solemnity of the room. I could not help but to be perturbed by the fly's disrespect. How could he simply carry on with his insignificant life, while the air itself was heavy with sorrow and mourning? As I approached the casket, I forced myself to look. I felt as though I was watching him sleep, like he would just wake up any moment. Unrelenting, the same annoying fly zoomed right over his folded hands. Why couldn't that fly have died instead of him? It seemed so unfair. As I watched the fly leave the casket, his hands caught my eyes. I could see blemishes, scars, calluses, and the wrinkles of time etched into his hands. The things those hands had done! They had held his first spoon, his first book, and his first crush's hand. Those hands had fired guns in World War II, halfway around the world. Those hands had taught me to dance, to walk backwards, and to enjoy life while it lasts, while it lasts. I paused for a moment, not sure what to do or what to feel. Then I realized that, for me, those hands represented not the past, but the future, a legacy handed down from him to me. It was as if our lives were the Olympic torch run, and it was my turn to carry the torch. It occurred to me at that moment that that is what he wanted me to do—carry on our family's venerable legacy. As I walked away from the casket, I glanced back one last time. I could only but glance at his hands and realize that those hands had done one last thing—left a permanent impression on my life that called me to move forward into a new beginning, carrying the torch, our torch.

Chapter One

Handprints of Family

Sibling Rivalry
Elliott Todd
Thurman Francis Arts Academy, Grade 7

The memory to my brain still clings
Of the time Brad wanted to fling
My shorts on the ceiling fan
All part of his superior plan

On the second floor he stood
Knowing he could stop me, yes he would
When I walked in I was not aware
So then my eyes did not flare

I walked up to the balcony, to where he was
But I did not see the shorts because
I was facing the other way
Could I see them? I could not say

I then saw them on the fan
And I realized part of his premium plan
I tried to reach then, but I was not tall
However, I was careful so I would not fall

He flew down the stairs to the switch for the fan
And finally, I realized the rest of his plan
I glared at him, and he smirked at me
I had to fight, for I could not flee

The final confrontation, just him and me
And I knew I would have the victory
Then I heard a commanding voice
My victory by Mom's choice

"Get Eli's shorts off the fan,
and you're grounded for trying that plan."
He turned on the fan and the shorts fell to the floor
Sulking, he turned and walked out the door.

Marigolds and Asters
Millie Harrison
McFadden School of Excellence, Grade 6

Dear Gigi,

I'd been thinking, we never see each other much anymore. I miss you so much, even though you're just an hour away. Memories flood my mind whenever I think of you. Singing of flying through the sky in my little blue swing. Rolling along in that old, rusted, red wagon with dear friend and cousin, Connor. Sitting in the front yard, we can make a rhyme, anytime. Baby Colby falling off the rocking horse. Kisses at arrival, sucking on the sugary, sweet orange slices. I don't remember a single time we didn't have those together.

"Here, have an orange slice."
"You're loosin' your britches!"
"Let me scratch your back."
"Come, sit in my lap even though your mama says you're too big."
"Do you know "Marigolds and Asters?" I sang that in school when I was just your age!"

Your old, friendly voice echoes through my head. You've done so much for me, the least I could do is write a little poem for you.

Grass is swaying in the front yard,
You begin to sing.
I begin to sing along,
Looking at the tree and the faded blue swing.

Marigolds and Asters!
You patted my hand to the beat,
Marigolds and Asters!
I felt like jumping up and stomping my little feet.

Help me catch those kitties, Gigi
They've come out of the barn again.
Hush, be quiet little child
Or they'll sneak back in their pen.

Where's my mommy?
I want Daddy!
How 'bout an orange slice instead?
Get them out of your head!

Little Millie, pull up your britches!
Little Millie, come snuggle with me.
Little Millie, let's go swing,
Or I'll help you climb up that old tree.

Marigolds and Asters!
Now patting my hand to the beat,
Marigolds and Asters!
I feel like jumping up and stomping my much bigger feet.

Love,
Millie

One of a Kind Relationship
Karson O'Bryan
Siegel Middle School, Grade 8

On December 1, 1995
My mom got a little surprise
For it was something that would change her life
Not one, but two baby girls
Kelsey and Karson
Chubby little babies with bright green eyes
There is no lie about the story I'm going to tell,
Of a one of a kind relationship

I love my twin with all my heart
She's been with me through thick and thin
And I know she always will be
She's one of a kind and a gorgeous girl
I would never let her leave
We have a one of a kind relationship
We may be different, but, hey, she's my sis

She and I fight, but in the end
I know we will mend
Without her, a part of me would be missing
No matter what happens,
She'll always be in my heart
What can I say,
That's what makes our one of a kind relationship

My Grandfather Thomas
Thomas Gray
Blackman Elementary School, Grade 3

      Although he's dead, my grandfather Thomas was a great man. I actually have never met him, but I do know a lot about him. First, his nickname was Tom. He flew in the Air Force in WWII. He flew in the B-17 Flying Fortress. Oh! I forgot to mention that he was the tail gunner when they were bombing Germany, and shooting down half of the German planes. He also joined the war at the early age of 18. His full name is Thomas Alexander Moore III. He was my mom's dad. The war started in 1941 and ended in 1945. He was born on July 1, 1925. He died in 1985 because of a heart attack. He was a hero! I wish I could have flown in the B-17 Flying Fortress in WWII. But alas, he died in 1985, so he died 16 years before I was born. I wish I could have just seen him once. He was a great pilot, and a great man of his word.

I Am Hurt
Sable Gilliland
Daniel McKee Alternative School, Grade 9

I am hurt
Not the hit by a car hurt
Not the kind of hurt you get when you step on a nail
But just hurt by the fact he let her hit me
Hurt by the fact he joined in
Hurt by the fact he hurt his own flesh and blood
For her
All for her
Daddy,why?

My Father
Abigail Woodson
Blackman Elementary School, Grade 5

My father's name was Robert Lee Woodson. He was in the Navy. I lost him when I was six years old. He was a person that I never thought I would lose. He was the greatest thing that ever happened to me. I loved him very much. I have so many precious memories of him and me. He would always read me a bedtime story. And he always played with me. When I was in baseball, he would never miss any of my baseball games or practice games. And he loved taking me places like to the park, movies, museums, and out of state. The best thing about my dad was that he would never let me down, and he was always there for my family and me.
HE WAS THE BEST FATHER I COULD EVER HAVE!

My Sister
Bryan Lopez
Blackman Elementary School, Grade 3

      Do you know who has made a difference in my life? It is my little sister Giselle. I was pretty thrilled when she was born. Do you want to know what I was thrilled about? When she was born, we bought her a stuffed animal. I took her animal away from her, and my mom and dad have a picture of me taking the animal from her. She thought it was funny!
      Once when she turned five, Giselle started playing video games with me. I pretty much trained her how to play them. She did a great job. She is a good sister but sometimes she cheats when we play tic-tac-toe on paper! That's who has made a difference in my life!

My Mom
Krysta Forsberg
Blackman Elementary School, Grade 3

      My mom helps me do a lot of stuff like clean my room, do my laundry, my homework, and put my clothes away. She is so funny; that is why I laugh a lot at home. She is so awesome to my family and me. She is also cool, but only some of the time. She plays hangman with my family and me too. I love her so much. She rocks!

Family Trip
Alexander Salvatore
Blackman Elementary School, Grade 1

My heart is happy when I visit my family. This makes me happy because I am with my cousins. I git to play golf. It is a blast!

Handprints on My Heart
Jayen Patel
Blackman Elementary School, Grade 1

My heart feels happy when my brother laughs at me.

Son's Love
Benjamin Bishop
Blackman Elementary School, Grade 1

I love my mom and dad.
I love thim because they are nis.

Family
Alyssa Bolton
Blackman Elementary School, Grade 4

Fantastic
Amazing
My heroes
Intelligent
Loving
Yes, my family means the world to me.

Handprints on My Heart
Kylie Tarver
Blackman Elementary School, Grade 1

I love my dad
and he loves
me that is
what maks
me fel happy.

What Makes My Heart Happy
Zachary Stong
Blackman Elementary School, Grade 1

My berother makes my hart happy becus he looks at me and I love him.

The Specialist Mom
Alyssa Mealer
Blackman Elementary School, Grade 3

    Do you know someone that helps you with a lot of things? My mom is the one that helps me with a lot of things. She helps me with stuff like my homework, and doing class projects. She taught me how to eat and talk. She also buys me food, clothes, and all kinds of other things. She does tons of things for me.
    The number one reason why she is so special to me is because she loves me. She's as pretty and sweet as an angel. She's the coolest mom ever! My mom always makes me happy when I'm sad. She also takes care of me when I'm sick and gives me medicine.
    Sometimes we can get mad at each other, but in the end we always figure it out. When I'm sad crying in my room, she always comes and tells me it will be all right, and makes me happy. My mom loves me, and, of course, I love her.

My Brother Drew
Ashley Perhac
Blackman Elementary School, Grade 3

Bothers me a lot
Responsible
Other people like him
Taller than me
Hockey player
Emotional
Reads to me sometimes at night

Memories of Grandpa Vanek
Jessie Kearney
Blackman Elementary School, Grade 3

My Grandpa Vanek was very sweet. He gave me candy and other treats. He swung me around off my feet until I fell asleep. This is what I think of him.

Great
Read to me
Acted like a puppy
Not here any more
Didn't say bad words
Polite
And made the best pancakes

Very loving
And had a tickly beard and mustache
Not mean
Every time he smiled, I laughed.
Kind

Handprints
Sivilay Nick Chanthaseng
Blackman Elementary School, Grade 2

My handprint on my heart is my dad because he is saving Tennessee, and that is why I chose him. He's in the Army so I will put faith in him and I will send something to him and that is why I pick him.

Dear Dad
Erika Easterly
Rock Springs Middle School, Grade 6

Dear Dad,
   I miss you very much. It is hard to believe that you are in Kuwait. Mom, Adam, Duke and I all miss you. It is hard for me to sleep some nights without knowing you are there.
   I have been getting ready for my eleventh birthday. I know it won't be the same without you here to help celebrate. Mom has been setting up a web-cam so we can see each other over the internet.
   Adam has been upset. Even though he doesn't show it, his heart is crying out. Even Duke is sad. He drags around the house. Just because he is a dog, doesn't mea n he can't tell when someone is gone. I have been writing things about you being so far away, things that make me feel better.
   I can't wait 'til you get back. I hope we get to celebrate together. No matter how far away you are, no matter how long you are gone, I always think of you. When you get back in February, we can celebrate a little bit of Christmas then. We all miss you so very much.

Your best pal,
Erika

When My Brother Came Along
Gracie Range
Blackman Elementary School, Grade 3

   My brother came into this world on May 29, 2009. He was born at StoneCrest Hospital in Smyrna, Tennessee. It was the best day of my life. I had a little brother! It was so exciting! I came in the room and saw him and he looked just like me. I hugged him and loved on him. He's growing up now. He is five months old. He is such a joy!

The Letter I Can Never Send
Mariah Smith
Rock Springs Middle School, Grade 6

So sweet!!

Dear Granddaddy J. Smith,

    This is Mariah Nicole Smith, your granddaughter who loves you dearly, even though I never knew you. I have heard stories about you from Chelsea, Kaleigh, Stephen, Mom, Daddy, and Uncle Jeff ever since I was a little girl. Miff talks about you the most.

    They tell me, when I ask, about how you would say how beautiful I was, and how you never put me down. You loved me from the start. Even though I was only a baby when you met me, and you only held me once before you died, you still did.

    Now your spirit guides me everywhere I go; every step, every move, every word I say, you're there.

    Do you want to know what my number one goal is now? It is to make it to heaven, meet with you, and tell you how much I love you, and how much you mean to me. From the start, you left handprints on my heart.

I love you forever,
Mariah Smith
(your loving granddaughter)

Handprint on My Heart
Bekkah Riley
Christiana Middle School, Grade 6

Can you compare to her sweet love?
The mother who has helped me when times are tough,
She always forgives and never forgets.
Can you compare to the best mother yet?
She is my inspiration,
My heart and my soul,
She is always there to the end, right from the start.
Can you compare to her loving heart?
She allows pity, not shame,
She can lasso your heart, wild not tame
She could roam free, but she chooses me.
Can you compare to her everlasting love?
She will conquer your mind and speak of above,
You would say her love is an addiction,
A bond that never breaks.
But one thing that will never depart,
Is that she leaves a handprint on my heart.

He Leaves a Handprint on My Heart
Erika Dean
Christiana Middle School, Grade 7

A small gift that seems so innocent,
I feel more superior than he,
But he has a job, you know
And that is bothering me.

We have many disagreements,
We bicker and we fight.
I say he did it,
He says I am not right.

Still, I have to love him,
And care for him too.
Because he is my little brother,
And it is what I have to do.

Even though he annoys me,
He sometimes acts quite fair.
He wants to show off to me
And he loves to share.

Even if he does not seem like one,
He is a good, loving brother.
He leaves a handprint on my heart.
And we care for one another.
He leaves a handprint on my heart.

Handprint on My Heart

Peri Watson
Christiana Middle School, Grade 6

There are people who are dear to me
People who are close to me
People whom I love and care about
But one of them, my mom
Has changed me in many ways.
She has opened many doors for me
And loved me all her life
She held me in her arms when I was a child
Read stories to me at night
She sang lullabies as I closed my eyes
Kissed my ouchies when I fell down
She helped me up again and again
Telling me "it is okay"
I can try again tomorrow.
And even still today
She will hold me in her arms
And kiss me goodnight
It always makes me feel good inside
And leaves a handprint on my heart.

A.J. Taylor • Siegel High School • Grade 11

You Left a Handprint on My Heart
Rachel Smetana
Christiana Middle School, Grade 6

>I wept and wept,
>The day you left,
>But even though it was sad,
>You gave me something,
>Made me stronger,
>Helped me grow.
>Even though you are not here anymore,
>You left a handprint on my heart.
>You never let me down,
>You were always there,
>To be serious,
>Or just to joke around.
>Even though you are not here anymore
>You left a handprint on my heart.
>You loved me unconditionally,
>That was something I could see
>No matter what happened,
>I could talk to you,
>And you would help me.
>Even though you are not here anymore,
>You left a handprint on my heart.
>Even though we are now far away
>You are with me every step of the way.
>I have always loved you, Grandma; I always will.
>And even though you are not here anymore,
>You left a handprint on my heart.

Family
Collin Gabel
Cedar Grove Elementary School, Grade 1

I have a big family and it is fun. We play games together like Monopoly, hide-and-seek, and Sorry. We help each other. My parents help me with my homework. I help them clean and feed the cats. We hug one another a lot in my family. My favorite thing is they love me and I love them.

Handprints on My Heart
Diamond Morrison
Central Middle School, Grade 8

Dear Mom,

I love you so much, but I can't live here with you anymore. My life is not the same here. I can't do the things I usually did in Cleveland. Mom, I really miss being around my family, and I really miss my best friend. I need to go back to Cleveland, so I can stop being miserable here. Tennessee is just not for me. Don't you miss your best friend and your family? I know I do. I really miss my daddy, and I am really unhappy here. Please, Mom, let me go back to Cleveland.

Love always,
Diamond Morrison

P.S. I love you!

My Family and Me
Alyssa Watson
Blackman Middle School, Grade 6

    My sister, my parents, and my grandparents all have something in common. They all have left handprints on my heart. Whether it is loving me or helping me with my homework, it just leaves handprints on my heart. Like them, I leave handprints on their hearts, by helping my sister with her homework and helping my mom cook. A lot of people have left handprints on my hearts.

My Brother
Gabe Martin
Blackman Middle School, Grade 7

My brother was there
for the good times and the bad.
We didn't always get along,
and this makes me truly sad.
We both regret it,
all those times we got mad.
He is all grown up now,
recently becoming a high school grad.
He visits from time to time,
and this makes me very glad.
I love my brother, and I'm not the only one
so do my mom and dad.

A Marine's Life
Shelby Eberwein
Central Middle School, Grade 8

Sometimes I wonder why
Things have gotten this bad

And when I think of 9/11
It always makes me sad

Knowing we have family there
Fighting for us all

They'll stay there until the end,
Standing brave and tall

Their hearts now cold as ice,
Watching their friends die

BOOM is what they hear,
Before they start to sigh

Until it's over we'll keep writing
And hoping for the best

Every day closer to the day
They pass their test

When the plane lands and
They walk off safe and sound

They'll be a little different
From the new life they have found.

Dedicated to my cousin
Brandon Lantrip
U.S. Marine

Searching
Amanda Ward
Blackman Middle School, Grade 8

  My eyes are exhausted. I have no more energy. I have no more tears. Life seems to be like a storm around me, swallowing me whole. I have lost all hope. Any source of love, any source of comfort, any strand of promise has been stripped from me. All my plans have been washed away in this never-ending river, and they are never coming back.
  My soul is trying. Trying to find a sliver. A sliver of hope to hold on to.
  What am I supposed to do? I need someone to direct me. I need someone to tell me where to go. I need help. I'm so confused. I feel like everything that I had once known and been familiar with is of no value anymore. Everything that I have ever been through, everything that I have learned....Nothing.
  My life is an ocean's wave. One unbearable expectation after the next...Forever.
  I am such a mess. I feel like I should just give up. A pile of broken dreams. A puddle of tears. That's all that's left of me.
  I feel like a part of me has left. Moved away. The rest of me lay here. Torn. Shattered into a thousand pieces, and I can't figure out how to gather myself together again.
  Taking the next step is like climbing a mountain. It requires enormous amounts of courage. It takes everything I have. My last breath. My last hope of things going back to normal. I could just stay where I am. Cling on with all I am to this ledge. But sometimes, you get to the point where staying where you are is more painful than climbing that mountain in front of you.

  When I was searching for someone to lean on, when I was desperately seeking for someone to climb those mountains with me, you were always there. You picked me up and carried me through chapters in my life where I felt that I didn't have a sliver of hope.
  I needed someone to direct me, and you were there. I needed someone to tell me what to do next, and you gave me a map. I needed someone to comfort me and tell me that everything was going to be okay, and you did. When I felt like smiling was impossible, you made me laugh out loud. You've been by my side through all of the difficult seasons of my life, and I have a feeling that you always will be. You freed me from the chains of my burdens that I carried for so long. You told me to always put my trust in the Lord, and I will never be able to thank you enough. You mean so much to me, even if I have said the opposite to you before. You will never know how awful I feel about that. You never deserved it. You have always known what's best for me, sometimes even more than myself. You have been the best dad a girl could ever dream about. Thank you. Thank you so much for picking me up and dusting me off. Thank you for always loving me, though I will never be able to understand why. Thank you.

I love you, Dad.

Handprints on My Heart
Allison Howard
Blackman Middle School, Grade 8

You leave your handprints on my heart
Even though we're far apart.

I need you in my life today.
The thought of you won't go away.

I hear the stories of your days
And though it seems as but a haze.

Your life was a great example
I live to be like you.

Though we never met face to face,
Somehow God made a way.

Our hearts are close together
And will be till the end.

Your family, we miss you dearly,
But we live for that day.

We'll see you up in heaven
When our time has come.

I promise I won't stop loving you
Even to that day.

Grandma, your handprint is on my heart.

Little Kaiden Carter
Christian Sims
Blackman Middle School, Grade 8

Sitting in a waiting room overnight after a four-hour drive.
Waiting for an update.
Nothing but sounds of silence coming from the empty waiting room.
We start to get restless until he comes barging through the door,
My brother.
He informs us that everything is all right.
He tells us to go and get some rest.
Later that evening we pull into the busy parking lot of the hospital.
We walk through the sliding glass doors to meet my exhausted brother.
He leads us up into a quiet hospital room.
I sit down as my mom starts crying and lays a warm blanket into my arms.
I still remember the sweet looks on little Kaiden Carter's face.
The calm, slow movement from my nephew's legs.
I couldn't believe how small his little hands were.
Little Kaiden Carter.

My Granny Loved to Fish
Spencer Hutchins
Blackman Middle School, Grade 7

I wish I had had my Granny longer,
she died when I was young.
If I had had my Granny longer,
I know we would've had fun.

I have a picture of her holding me,
when we were on her boat.
She was helping me to fish,
it was cold, and we both were wearing our coats.

One day my Granny got sick,
and then she passed away.
I know that she is in heaven,
probably fishing every day.

Although I miss my Granny,
I try not to be blue.
Fishing was her favorite pastime,
and now, thanks to her, I love to fish too!

A Mother Like You
Torryn Windrow
Blackman Middle School, Grade 7

How to describe a mother like you…
What does one say; what does one do?

Mention the warmth, your unselfish ways…
Your love that brings joy to all of our days.

How to give praise for your sweet tenderness…
For the wonderful traits that only angels possess.

Somehow I have not the words to reveal…
The depth of my love and the affection that I feel.

I will just have to hope that you will understand…
You always do, Mother; that's why you are so grand.

Grandma
Isabelle Hydrick
Barfield Elementary School, Grade 4

Grandma is so sweet. She always makes me smile especially when I haven't seen her in a long time. She makes me very happy, but I still love Pappy too. She is the greatest person in the whole world. When I am crying, she knows that I am not lying. She knows that I am really very sad and she does not get mad. She is the most fantastic, terrific, greatest, and most wonderfully fabulous person in the whole world.

For My Mommy
Christina Wells
Oakland High School, Grade 12

In my darkest hour
At my first tear
Though some may try to my soul devour,
You will always to me be near

From my first cry
To life's first walk
Though I may leave in the sweet by and by
It is to you I always come to talk.

When I'm so depressed I can't bear to stand
When exhaustion takes over the spirit of my being
You alone are my encouraging hand
On you can I always lean.

No matter what I've done
Even after all the bridges I burn
When I'm through walking on the sun
To you I will always return.

You're my best friend
And of my life you have the largest part.
My love for you will never end.
You've made the biggest handprint on my heart.

Parents
Jessica Polsinelli
Oakland High School, Grade 12

Person who leaves a handprint on my heart
Affectionate
Realistic
Enlightening
Nurturing
Trustworthy
Security

My Grandma
Patrick Cardel
McFadden School of Excellence, Grade 8

The soft rustle of the tranquil hammock, the loving hug that always finds its way to me, and the never-ending care are some things that I remember. My grandma was always there for me when I was young, and it is a joy to be around her. She was also one of my main caretakers when I was a baby. I love being with my grandma, but my favorite things about her are her care of me, staying at her house, and her support in my life.

When I was an infant, I could never be separated from my grandma. For many long hours, she would rock me in a hammock until I slowly fell asleep. I was also called her "Little Buddy" and grew up very close to her. My grandmother sang many songs to me, and I remember bouncing up and down on her lap. My grandma is great, and I also love being at her house.

At my grandmother's house there is always fun to be had. Nighttime brings about the need of a campfire. I can hear the intermittent noises of frogs in the spring, and it is relaxing to watch the fire slowly melt away into the night. Another wonderful part of my grandma's house is the massive pond full of fish. Watching the waterfall delicately trickle water back into the pond is always a glorious sight to behold. Although my grandmother's house is full of many free-time pleasures, my grandma is also very influential in supporting me in all my endeavors.

Lastly, my grandma encourages me to always try my best in everything I do. It is very encouraging to see her at my sports games and know that she is taking time out of her day to be with me. Along with sports, my grandma also commends me on my academic achievements. She is continually building me up, and I love all that she does for me. My grandma is very crucial in my life and always helps me dream for something better.

Above all, my grandmother has been there for me all my life. She is a friendly spirit to be around, and a day with her is never a wasted day. I appreciate all the experiences I have shared with her, and her support in my life is immeasurable. I love my grandma, and wherever I go, I can feel her love for me.

Handprint on My Heart
Carrington Creasy
McFadden School of Excellence, Grade 1

My mother touches my heart because she loves me.
She takes me wonderful places. We have lots of fun baking cupcakes and decorating them with sprinkles. My mom likes to read books to me at bedtime. My sister and I love to play games and eat pizza with her on girls' night. These are just a few ways my mom has made a handprint on my heart.

Grandma Ollie
Maggie Harris
McFadden School of Excellence, Grade 3

      My great-grandmother Ollie was a sweet, sweet lady. My mom would go over to her house all the time to spend the night. Her house always smelled like baking biscuits. If you were hungry at 12:00 at night, she would fix you cheeseburgers, macaroni, gravy biscuits, and jelly toast.
      She had a huge house and ten kids! She also had a handsome husband named Leander. He died of cancer before Grandma Ollie. She loved sweets. She would also keep a bowl of candy beside her bed. She would always cook up a big meal of lima beans, cheeseburgers, macaroni, gravy, biscuits, tater tots, and chocolate pie.
      When she went to bed every night, she would always put on a thick layer of lipstick and dangly earrings. She said it was because "you never know." Back then she might have to get up in the middle of the night to go help one of the family members deliver a baby.
      She died from a stroke before I was born. She was buried in a mausoleum because she didn't want to be in the dirt with the snakes and bugs. I wish I had had the chance to meet her but my family tells me I am a lot like her.

My Cousin
Jevon Lee
LaVergne Primary School, Grade 1

I wrestle with my cousin Joe Joe. We play with Transformers. We play basketball. We take a nap and eat pizza. We have so much fun!

Dear Ma
Macey Sweeton
Lascassas Elementary School, Grade 4

Dear Ma,
    I hope you know how much it means to me to have you here watching over me. You're the one I love no matter what. I hope you know it, too. I can always count on you. You're the best grandma I could ever wish to have. I want to be just like you when I grow up. You take me everywhere. I tell everyone about you. You always forgive me no matter what. My wish for Christmas is for you to always be happy. You've always given me whatever I wanted. I love you!

Thank you,
Macey

A Mother's Love
Shelby Follis
Lascassas Elementary School, Grade 7

    Do you ever feel you are missing something, like your heart is empty? Well, I have felt this horrid feeling. I now realize that what my heart was missing was a mother's sweet love. A mother's love is like a sweet ice cream cone given to you on a scorching summer day.
    The reason why I felt this emptiness was because my mother, Lara Christine Follis, passed away a month before I turned two years old, June, 14, 1999.It was a dreadful time for my father and me. We carried on though. We did pretty well, but I always knew something was missing.
    Luckily, when I turned four my father met a lovely young woman with an eight-year-old daughter. My father and the woman, Kristie, fell in love. Now I have a new mother and my heart is whole. I thank God every day that she came into my life. I now have that ice cream cone on a hot summer day.

My Dad
Bain Smith
Lascassas Elementary School, Grade 4

In 2003, my dad was sent to Iraq during "Desert Storm." He flew a C-130 carrying ammunition and supplies to the American soldiers in Iraq. They were fighting Sadaam Hussien. My dad camped for six months near the battlefield. When my dad was in Iraq, my mom had to deal with me because I was only three years old. I was sad because my dad was gone and missed some important stuff in my life, like the first time I changed my clothes by myself. When my dad came home, I was so happy to see him that I jumped over the wall and hugged my dad tight! You may have heard about my dad, his name is Major Alan Bain Smith. I am so proud of my dad.

Dear Papa
Taylor Robinson
Kittrell Elementary School, Grade 1

Dear Papa,
Have a very good Veterans Day. I like hearing your stories about being in the navy. Papa did you like your job? You must be very brave!

Love,
Taylor

My Parents
Katherine Kimball
Lascassas Elementary School, Grade 4

My parents have taught me many important things in my life like how to read, spell, cook, fish, and many more things. I am so thankful for them and their love. Their names are Trey and Kim. I don't know what I would do without them. Sometimes I get mad at them, but I will always love them. They are very important to my brothers and me. When my mom and I do something together, it is always special because we don't get to do things a lot. I love to do things with my dad. He is cool, fun, and exciting! On Christmas, they buy me presents. On Valentine's Day, my dad brings my mom and me chocolate. On Halloween, they buy me a costume. Sometimes, we go to our back field and have a picnic. We take our four-wheelers and ride around our new land. We sometimes take walks together or just sit on our front porch. Sometimes, I go to work with my dad. He works at Kelly Enterprises. When I go with him, we sometimes stop and eat breakfast. Then, we go eat lunch somewhere. When I'm with my mom, we go shopping. We buy clothes and shoes. Then we get something to eat for lunch. Wherever I am with my parents will always be special to me.

Lasagna
Kennedy Blackwood
Kittrell Elementary School, Grade 1

Dear Mom and Dad,
I love bote of you, and I love your spgete and tokos. I don't love your lsana.

Love,
Kennedy

My Grandma
Nicholas Mitchell
Kittrell Elementary School, Grade 2

My grandma is so kind. She has a smart, smart mind. She fought for my brother and me in court. No one can take us away.
We are with my sweet, sweet grandma forever and ever.

Bill
Mia Cortner
John Colemon Elementary School, Grade 5

Dedicated to my loving grandfather, Bill Bonner

Bill
Happy, brave, hardworking, smart
Grandfather of Mia, Hagan, and Emily
Who loved The United States of America, his family and working in his woodshop.
Who was afraid of his family getting hurt, the death of war, and jumping out of planes, but his fear did not stop him.
Who wanted to see a happy family, a happy country, and the land of God, Israel.
Resident of heaven
Bonner

Sandra
Alexis Goodson
John Colemon Elementary School, Grade 5

Sandra
Pretty, smart, energetic, intelligent
Grandmother of Alexis, Jordan, and Justin
Who loves grandkids, movies and me very much.
Who is afraid of snakes, spiders, and mice.
Who wants to see the beach, Hawaii, and her grandkids grow up.
Resident of Smyrna, Tennessee
Lawson

My Special Person
Lexy Curry
Rock Springs Elementary School, Grade 5

Have you ever had a person that is special to you? Well, I do. She has dark brown hair, light skin, dark brown eyes, and she is as beautiful as a princess. She is my mom. She is the best mom in the world, because she helps me with my homework and she takes care of me. I remember one time when I was very sick, and she took her time to care for me until I was better. Another time I had a lot of homework and she helped me until it was all finished. I think she is the coolest mom in the whole wide world, and that is why she is my special person.

Hand on My Heart
Carson Farley
Homer Pittard Campus School, Grade 6

Lots of things have left handprints on my heart. I made an acrostic poem to show how such wonderful things have made a big impact on my heart.

       Decorating the C**H**ristmas tree with my family.

          Playing bask**E**tball with my dad.

              Pl**A**ying with my dog, Lucy.

Laughing with my mothe**R.**

Mrs. Paul reading, *Where **T**he Red Fern Grows.*

And much, much more.

Role Model
Alexandria Moore
Rock Springs Elementary School, Grade 5

In loving memory of Matthew Anthony Battle

He was my grandfather; I was his "Little Nurse."
He had diabetes, and I helped give him insulin shots.
He liked to listen to records, and I liked to listen to his stories.
One rainy
       Miserable
              Sad
                     Afternoon….
I received THE phone call that caused me to have an anxiety attack.
My grandfather was taken to the hospital where he later died.
Tears
     Running
          Down
               My cheeks
He lives in my soul forever.

What's Special to Me!
Matthew Connors
Rock Springs Elementary School, Grade 5

There are several things that are special to me, but my father is one of the most special. He does so much for me, and I will always love him.

My dad has coached me in sports for more than six years. He has always supported me in whatever I do. He puts a lot of effort into making sure that I have fun. Even though he works many hours each week, he still helps me improve in sports.

My father has provided me with everything I have. He has worked hard, so that my family has a house to live in and food to eat. I am very fortunate to have such an amazing dad, because some kids can't say that.

We don't always agree on everything. We do have some arguments, but everything gets worked out. We are also very competitive. When we play games against each other, things get crazy, but it's all in fun.

I think I have the best dad ever! He will always love me, and my father is very special to me!

I Remember
Allison Hatfield
Rock Springs Middle School, Grade 7

I remember her smile
I remember her precious face
I remember her kind words
I remember her love for me
I remember her sweet, soft voice
I remember her care and forgiveness
I remember when she told me she would always be there
I remember the day she passed away
I remember my amazing aunt Rene
I remember, and I'll never forget

My Grandfather
Ashley Harper
Rock Springs Middle School, Grade 7

Jubilant joy
Exciting elder
Super grandfather
Safety crazy
Exaggerations were funny

Great guy
Willing to help
Important man
Needed in my life

My Brother
Dajiah Platt
Rock Springs Middle School, Grade 6

My brother really urks me.
He's just so annoying.
He shoots me with toy guns
But it's just his way of having fun.
I go to have fun, but he has to tag-a-long
And I always say, "No Way!"
He comes to me with questions that can wait another day.
But deep down I love him, and there's no doubt
That my crazy little brother
Is what this poem is about!

Dad, Will You Please Come Home?
Hailey Haraway
Rock Springs Middle School, Grade 6

Hailey's famous quote, "Someday my dad will get better
So that's why I'm writing this letter."

Dad,
Will you please come home?
We have been waiting for you like forever.
I don't know why you keep running from me and family.
I feel like you don't even want to be around me.
You have run away ever since I was just a baby.
You keep breaking my heart, and it hurts really badly.
I am not going to deal with this anymore.
I don't know you and you don't know me.
I have been growing older with my mom and God.
I am done and you can't stop me!
I am moving on.
Hope you understand.
I don't need you.
I have my mom and most importantly God to stay with me forever and always.
I don't need you.
I just don't.

Our Little Tradition
Maria Quaintance
Rock Springs Middle School, Grade 6

It's dark outside
As you tuck me into bed.
You ask me how my day was,
But I tell you this instead.
I say, "Daddy, I like you"
And you smiled ear-to-ear.
You leaned down and said slowly,
"I like you, too."
You said good night and turned out the lights
And from then on,
It became our little tradition.

Mom
Brandon Ray
Riverdale High School, Grade 12

The strong brilliance of a woman,
Her love for me a song.
She lays down her life for me.
I'm proud to call her mom.

I Miss You
Stephanie Davis
Riverdale High School, Grade 12

Twizzlers and soap operas
Cooking and singing
Disney movies and cuddling
Bedtime stories and rocking
Laughing and crying
Hugs and kisses
Teaching right and wrong
I miss you Grandma

For the Mothers of the Class of 2010
Lauren Hendrix
Riverdale High School, Grade 12

You've left handprints on my heart,
Pride in my mind,
Ambitions in my soul,
And memories to last a lifetime.

Thank you for your love,
And thank you for your life.
Thank you for your support,
And thank you for all the advice.

If only you knew how much you mean to me
And how everything you do matters.
You've prepared me for the next phase
And everything that comes after.

I'm ready to take on this crazy world
And be out there on my own
But one thing I'll always know is
You'll be there when I need to come home.

One Choice Can Change a Life
David Rice
Riverdale High School, Grade 12

A cross in the sky
Viewed through a window
A heavily barred window

A dream in the night
That leads through a door
A heavily barred door

A son who dreams
An impossible dream
And finds a way home

A dream that leads
To a long lost friend
Who lives far away

A decision in the dark
That makes the dark grow bight
And I followed the light
To an impossible goal

An unbeatable challenge
Was beaten
When you attack it
the fathers and I
With everything you have

        A Reunion
        That means
        A Division

        A Division
        That means
        A Reunion
        They are one

        The death of a life
        Means the beginning of another
        And both are mine

        One Night
        One Dream
        One Choice
        Can change a life forever

        Two Fathers
        One Above
        One Beside
        Both are Mine

        To the family I lost and
        gained, one above and one beside

A Mother's Love
Austin Bradford
Riverdale High School, Grade 12

I awoke one morning with blankets of snow hugging the ground
I walked outside to see the great sight, to see the winter animals' handprints all around

At only nine years of age, it was a miraculous sight
Anxious for the morning, I slept little through the night

This Christmas was the best, with all of the joy and cheer
Not because of the toys, but because of all the love to adhere

I told my mother I loved her, not for all the material things that come from a cart,
But for all the love she has for me, and the handprint she left on my heart.

My Family in 2008
Tyler Stout
Homer Pittard Campus School, Grade 1

      In 2008 I had a good family. It was kind of fun. I had two pets. Their names were Spike and Shadow. I loved them. They were guinea pigs. My Dad was strong. He could almost lift up my whole bed. He sometimes liked to lift weights. My brother liked to play outside. We liked to play baseball with each other. My Mom liked to go on lots of walks. She was strong like my Dad. I loved my family and they loved me. The end.

To My Grandma Who Changed My Life
Karsen Daniel
Eagleville School, Grade 3

The one I love with all my might.
The one I'm thinking of tonight.
The one that helps me make things right.
The one that I long to kiss goodnight.
The one I dream of when I sleep at night.
The one I think of when I hug my pillow tight.
The one that makes me happy when she comes into my sight.
The one I'm not giving up without a fight.

Just My Daddy and Me
Morgan Herring
Thurman Francis Arts Academy, Grade 2

A special time to me is when I get to do things with my daddy—*just* my daddy and me.
I have two little sisters, so it doesn't happen that often.
Some of my favorite things to do with my daddy are to go golfing and hunting.
I had to wait until I was five to go hunting. I also got to go to a golf practice with him.
I feel extra special when it is just the two of us.

A Handprint on My Heart
Krista Martin
Eagleville School, Grade 8

    I have many handprints that are on my heart, but there is one in particular which comes to mind. My papa was a strong, independent, and kind man. At least he was to me. He was my best friend and he will always be that. No one can replace him. He used to set me on the table and we'd play cards, and, of course, get in trouble for it. Mema would tell me to get down and Momma said that we knew better. Then, he'd set me right back up there just to get on their nerves.

    He had his bullying moments trying to get Mema and Momma worked up. The day he died we were having a yard sale. Momma had told me to go ask Papa if we could have some paper, then I went back to his room to ask. When I got back there, there he was. That is, I thought he was asleep. I grabbed a couple of sheets of paper and ran outside to my Mema. I told her he wouldn't get up and she went back to get him. The next thing I knew she came running outside yelling, "Call an ambulance, Kelley's dead!" I was in shock! I didn't know what to do. My mom ran inside and I just stood there like I was waiting for him to come out unharmed, but he never did. He came out on a stretcher just lying there not moving, not breathing. Then the unspeakable happened. The doctors pronounced him dead. He had died in the middle of the night from a heart attack, and I had found him that morning.

    When it was time for his funeral I couldn't even go into the room. My dad ended up carrying me. When I saw him, I started crying. Although he was lying there exceedingly peaceful with all his Titans trinkets, I couldn't look at him! I couldn't be strong like everyone said to do. My one and only true best friend had died and I was never going to see him again until I died myself. That was the worst day of my life! Everyone said they understood but no one could understand my pain or the weight on my heart.

    I think God told my Papa he was going to die because the week before he called everyone he had ever been mean to or hurt in some way and apologized. He knew it was his time and he was ready. Now I know he watches over me every day, and I will see him again. He'll meet me at the "Pearly Gates" and walk with me on the "golden streets beside the crystal sea!" That makes everything I've been through worthwhile! My Papa always told me how much he loved my two cousins and me. We were his prized possessions! I used to think I could hear him at night like he was in the room saying, "Good night, I love you!" Some days I used to go inside Mema's house and think he was going to be there waiting! Now I know that that won't ever happen! My mom and dad have stayed up through endless nights with me while I sat and cried. Even though I'm slowly loosing the sound of his voice, his smell, and his touch, he's still in my heart!

Handprints on My Heart
Trevor Sharber
Eagleville School, Grade 3

My name is Trevor Sharber, and I am adopted. My mom and dad were happy when they got me. I have a big brother and sister. I think my family is awesome! I am glad they got me.
My family cares about me a lot. They always help me when I need them. They are always there for me. They think I am special. I know some other kids don't have moms and dads. I feel sad for them. I hope they get a family, and they are happy just like me!
My mom says I was always in her heart. So, I guess my handprints were there, too.

My Brother
Logan Moore
Eagleville School, Grade 3

I have a brother named Jeremy. He is in the United States Air Force. He really means a lot to me. Sometimes when he comes home for the weekend, we play football together. Sometimes he has to leave, and I miss him a lot when he has to go. Sometimes when he is supposed to come home he doesn't. Jeremy doesn't like it because some of his Air Force friends do not follow the rules. That means Jeremy can't come home. I am really sad when he can't come. I really do miss him, and I love him!

My Unborn Niece
Gracie Walden
Wilson Elementary School, Grade 5

My little niece, kicking away,
Stuck inside her mom's tummy all day.
I feel her little foot bump against my hand,
I can't wait until she can finally stand.
Her mom's stomach is as round as a ball,
She'll be so cute when she can finally crawl.
Even when she is a newborn,
If we were separated I would be torn.
I love her so much, even though I can't see her,
I definitely can't wait to meet her.

My Other
Kayla Stiles
Eagleville School, Grade 6

Even though I never knew you, I love you very much.
When I was little, you would visit me in my dreams.
And we would talk and play.

Even today when there is a beam of light in my dream,
I know it is probably you watching over me.

I can just imagine what it would be like if you were here,
But I can only imagine.

Mom and Dad would have named you Nathan,
But now I have a younger brother with that name.
I know you would love our family of six.

You will always be in my heart,
And I love you very much.
I can't wait until we are reunited once again.

In memory of my unborn twin.

A Place I Love
Elizabeth Nelson
McFadden School of Excellence, Kindergarten

I love to go to my Gramos hose and fed the dog. Where else can you ped dogs in pese?

Move On
David Najera
Wilson Elementary School, Grade 5

My grandma has cancer and she just might die,
The day I heard of this I wanted to cry.
I know I'm not the only one who has this pain,
If you don't move on it'll drive you insane.
Like most I'm one of those, but I learned to move on,
She's like my second mother, and I'm like her son.

My Sister
Sarah Merritt
Wilson Elementary School, Grade 1

My sister died when she was eight years old. I miss her very much. I remember playing on the playground with her when I was four.

My Family
Austin Gamble
Wilson Elementary School, Grade 1

I love my family. My family is really fun. My dad and I like to go hunting together. My mom and I like to read books together. My sister and I like to play games together. It's fun to be together as a family.

On My Dad's Birthday
Ava Palmer
Wilson Elementary School, Grade 1

On my dad's birthday, my Mom and I baked a cake for Dad. My sister was a big help! When my dad got home he was surprised. He loved the cake so much it was gone in a second!

Grandpa
Peyton Milam
Brown's Chapel Elementary, Grade 5

Great and loving person
Really touched my heart
Awesome at camping
Navy soldier
Depend on him
Played with us
Awesome friend and grandpa

My Inspiration
Victoria Clowers
Brown's Chapel Elementary School, Grade 5

Dedicated to my Great-Grandmother, Waynett Quarles

The smell of your house,
The love in the air,
All the stories you have to tell.
The taste of your food,
The way you inspire me
With your love for every simple thing.
The way, on Christmas,
You know just what to get me.
How you enjoy
Every second with me.
When I hug you,
I don't want to let go.
I never want to leave you.
You never say never and you never give up.
That's why you are my inspiration, Grandma Quarles.

Big Mamaw
Grant York
Wilson Elementary School, Grade 2

Big Mamaw was the best. Some of the special memories I have of her are that she had lots of hugs for me, fried apples in the morning, and the best house. I love and miss her so much. She is still in my heart.

My Dad
Savanna Morrow
Brown's Chapel Elementary School, Grade 4

Does getting ice cream sound fun? Does going shopping sound even better? Well, that's what my dad and I used to do! He would do almost anything with me.

My dad and I always used to go to go U.S.A. We would ride go carts, play mini golf, and play the video games. We had a stupendous time with each other.

My dad and I would also go to Old Fort Park and play on the playground. He would push me on the tire swing, and right before we would go play we would go get some food and have picnics. My dad was full of joy and love and he spent it on my sister and me. We still love him from this very day forward.

My dad loved to cook, and I loved to help him. We would make all my favorites and eat them all up for lunch and dinner. He made the best spaghetti, toast, and mac-n-cheese. It was almost everything I'd eat when I went to my dad's.

My dad lives far away from me now and so we don't get to see each other often. I will always love him and he will always love me. He will always be in my mind. I will never forget the things we did together and hopefully he won't either.

My Mom
Caitlin Lister
Brown's Chapel Elementary School, Grade 4

Does your mom tell you that you can do anything? Mine does and she always has believed in whatever I do. And that's why I love her.

I didn't think I would be able to play softball, but my mom told me otherwise. She said that if I practiced enough every day I would be able to play and I would possibly be good. She has supported me every year I have played softball.

The same with choir. I thought I wasn't a very good singer because that is what my sister told me. She was always putting me down but my mom was there to build me right back up. My mom told me that if singing was what I wanted to do then that was what I should do. Now every time I get back from choir practice she asks me if I sang my heart out and asks if I had fun. It makes me feel like she actually cares and doesn't just come pick me up for no reason.

My mom knows that I will succeed. Even if I don't, she knows that I will try again and again until I finally get it right. She is the mom anybody would want. She wants us to succeed but she is not competitive, so it doesn't always have to be a first place trophy or a trophy at all. She just wants us to do our best at everything we try to do.

My mom always has faith in me. So no matter where I go, I will always be thinking of her for all the wonderful things she ha taught me. She is the best mom in the world!

My Family
Hayden Rumpf
Walter Hill Elementary School, Grade 2

I love my family. Dad, Mom, my baby brother, sister, and I have fun. We go to the park, beach, pool, restaurants, and to Carolina to see Maw Maw and Pa Paw. We try to make every day special!

My Family
Amber Hurt
Walter Hill Elementary School, Grade 2

I love my family.
My family loves me.
We all love each other.
They are all nice to me.

Christina Vongsiharath • Blackman Elementary School • Grade 1

She Helps Me Fly
Crystal Meadors
Siegel Middle School, Grade 8

She makes me laugh,
She makes me cry.
She pulls me down,
She helps me fly.

I needn't worry
When she's around.
She pulls me up
When I am down.

But when she's mean
There's a piece of art,
Made of handprints
Slapped on my heart.

She'll make me cry;
I'll be mad for a while.
But then she'll laugh,
And it makes me smile.

She pulls me through
Even the darkest days.
She helps me walk,
So I can find my way.

If I mess up,
She's there for me.
She always says,
"Be the best you can be."

She never laughs
At the things I do.
Instead she helps,
Until I'm through.

When life gets tough,
She becomes my friend.
She stays with me,
From beginning to end.

Although we fight
Like sisters would,
Because of her
I've been changed for good.

I Remember
Yeilen Rodriquz
Siegel Middle School, Grade 8

I remember when my grandmother
read me a story from her favorite book.
I remember how she made me giggle and laugh.
I remember her facial expressions with every line she read.
I remember her in bed very sick.
I remember when she passed away; my tears falling on her pillow.
As the weeks passed by and there was no sign of that book she use to read to me. I searched under her bed and found a box with all of the pictures we took together and delightedly under them I found the book. Inside was a note that said 'I will always remember you."

Eddie
Kaley Humphrey
Siegel High School, Grade 12

I remember as children we would laugh and play
With the "monster" that chased us around and away.
He hugged so tightly when we said goodbye
But never let us see him cry.
Every summer he'd take us out
To swimming, tennis, all about.
Even jobs he did for friends,
He'd take us with him there and then.
That exuberant man with a gapped tooth grin
Had a servant's heart and committed no sin.
Why did cancer choose to victimize one
So much more than a husband, a father, a son?
We may ask why and not comprehend
The exclusion of this man and friend,
But when my grief arrives back at the start,
I find comfort for his handprint is there on my heart.

Her Knitting
Tori Hawkins
Siegel High School, Grade 10

Wrinkled fingers cascade over my grandmother's heart
Once young and youthful as a summer's day
Now sit in her lap as her would has fallen apart
I look outside and hear thunder

Her thinning hair catches a breeze as she looks up at me
And I can see the days of childhood
Running through flower pastures and her golden locks flirting with bees
But then I look and the hair is white string again

Grandma gracefully moves her scarred feet
And although her feet are covered in slippers
I can see the pain as if it were the day her parents were taken away in the heat
Again and again as she glides to her seat

Grandma then puts her in the light and I see the sapphire ring
Shining as if it were the day Grandpa had given it to her
Twenty and young was she, and sass that hurt like a new bee sting
Grandma moves her fingers once more and I see the rust on the rim

She speaks with such cordialness it makes me wonder
Is this the voice that sang and made church come alive?
But mom tells me it's the voice she speaks with since a heart attack took Grandpa asunder
Then Grandma goes back to knitting and purses her mouth shut

Her knitting comes to an end and so does her story
Her body stops moving and does nothing at all
I cry out but not inch moves in glory
Then I look at my hair and wonder
Will there ever be a day when my fingers will cascade over my heart
And I go down in thunder?

Pap

Molly Underwood
Siegel High School, Grade 10

Pap, not Grandpa, Papaw, or Pa, sits
In his favorite chair in the warm air and smiles
To Fred his beloved dog or some would call fat, but still wonderful.
He laughs as he drinks his coffee in the early morning with my nana
Outside by his side.

I remember his names for things and how he smelled; I thought it was wonderful
His false teeth coming out when he smiled,
I thought it was the funniest thing, we would laugh and sit
Under the shade of the trees with my family outside
The world in our own.

I remember waking up on Christmas morning,
The anticipation of the day ahead was always wonderful,
Waiting, waiting, for him to get ready; it was always
Good, the smell of his cologne (Old Spice, nothing else).
In his chair in the room he sits

Playing solitaire, sitting, the happiest man in the world
Because of his love for God is so clear.
I see him reading with a magnifying glass and patiently reading
And listening to God and he smiles;
He knows that he will be with his mom and daddy soon.

I remember how he would tell us stories, how he would sit
At the table and pray the Lord's Prayer with much sincerity,
An old man who loved to watch westerns,
And his children grow tall and strong, and see
Them grow up; watch his children make it in life

He has nine lives, I believe, he lives and lives
But now he has gotten tired; he is content and wonderful
Thoughts seep deeply in his head,
He sees his puppy and his wife and his family, but lets it stay on this side
He is going to the other with the Father, and he finally sits

On the porch with a glass of tea and a cigarette.
The scent of tobacco lingers in the air, and there he is always with a smile
I see that he is coming, I grin because I know that he is here and I sit
By his bright heart, one you could see from miles away.
One you knew was always there.

I remember him as loving,
The most charming man I have ever known, beside
Me, he thinks of something else to make me giggle, he knows I love to smile,
And I laugh till my side hurts,
But not too badly. There is always room for more.

I remember his trucks (no, nun nuns according to John) and nana
Loving him with all her heart as she has been by his side
For a very long time. I lost track at forty years, I smile
At the sweet man I get to call Grandfather, who sits
In his chair holding Fred and rubbing his belly. It's wonderful.

When one of your deepest wishes
Is to pay for some stranger's groceries, and that he sits
On the porch telling us this and smiles with much sincerity
He smiles and laughs and says, "Molly says that she loves me very much."
He says that with the proudest look on his face; I know he loves me, too.

I say that's right I do love you, with all my heart,
By my side, he looks at me with tired but loving eyes
And says I love you, too.

Why I Love U
Nathan Price
Siegel Middle School, Grade 7

I have six brothers and sisters and I love all of them. The one closest to my heart has to be my little brother Dylan. The reason he's so close is because he's gone and can't come back.

Dylan died fours years ago when he was three months old. There is not one day that I don't think about him. I can still remember his soft giggle. I would tickle him in the stomach and he would go insane with laughter.

I knew he loved me because when I held him he never cried, mainly because I always had a bottle in his mouth. If he ever fell asleep in my arms, I had to put him in his crib. When I laid him down he'd always yawn and wiggle around until he was comfortable.

I had a special alarm clock, but it wasn't one that you couldn't wind up or reset or snooze. Dylan always got up early in the morning. He was ready to eat and I was ready to feed. I don't know why but anytime someone fed him he would always hold onto to your finger and you couldn't get it out if you tried.

It surprises me how much I know about him when I didn't know him for a long time. I miss him so much and can't stop thinking about him no matter how old I get and hopefully never will.

My Brother
Nicole Gardner
Siegel Middle School, Grade 7

You are my brother
One of three
Back from overseas

I worried for you
Every morning
And prayed every night

You opened my eyes
From a blind sleep
To a whole new world

Nothing bad ever
Befalls on you
That is as I thought

But as I soon learned
Things could happen
To you or to me

Tragedy occurred
That injured you
Proof still lives today

I thank God daily
For bringing you
Home to us, to me

But finally you
Are home for good
Safe and sound with us

You are my brother
One of three
Back from overseas

Her Survival Story
Katie Stotler
Siegel Middle School, Grade 8

When I was little, my mother and I used to crank up the stereo and dance around the house as if we were idiots. Some days, she would let me jump onto the coffee table and just go wild. That's when everything was all right. Things can flash right before your eyes. My advice is that you slow down and take a look around, because by the time you realize how lucky you are to have something or someone so close to you, they could be gone in an instant. You will regret not taking your time to make sure that you're living each day to the fullest. Something happened to me. It's something I will never forget. I can still remember all of these events like they happened yesterday. Time flies so fast, and I can't believe it has been five years since everything in my life turned completely upside down. Countless days sitting impatiently, wait for results is what made me want all the madness to end. It's terrible to have to see a loved one in so much misery, especially my best friend, my hero, my remarkable mother. It all started on a cool December night. The atmosphere of Christmas lingered around our home. The lights of the fire truck gleamed on my bedroom window. The earsplitting siren of the ambulance came to a stop as soon as various people where running inside. Being a child, I had no idea what was happening and cried myself into what seemed like an endless slumber. I awoke feeling disoriented about everything that had happened just the night before. Later, finding out my mother was rushed to the hospital while having three heart attacks, I could not consider what I heard was true. One person should never have to spend two weeks in ICU, let alone stuck in a bed with nothing to do. Recovery soon took its place. The family had our Christmas just like always, with no concerns. Three short years later we found ourselves moving out of our home of eleven wonderful years and buying a new house in Murfreesboro, Tennessee. I was entering the sixth grade, and my brother, Keith, was entering his first year of college at MTSU. My father had just scored a new job as a sales manager with Xerox for Tennessee. Getting used to our daily routine was fairly easy, until things that shouldn't ever happen to someone, happened to us. During the next three years my mother was diagnosed with three different types of cancer, colon-rectal, rectal, and brain cancer. Of course, these times were some of the most challenging my family had ever know. My mother always told me that no matter what happened, I was always the best thing that has ever happened to her, and that I mean the world to me. When she had colon-rectal cancer, they had the tumor removed about two weeks after she had been diagnosed. A month later, a ventricular shunt was put into her chest for six months of chemotherapy. My mother, grandmother, brother, and I went back and forth to the hospital while my mother was being treated. Rectal cancer was pretty much the same as before, but instead they treated her by radiation. The first two rounds of cancer weren't as alarming as when my mother had brain cancer. Watching the nurse take her into surgery to remove the tumor, knowing that I might not be able to see her heart-warming smile ever again was the worst thing my eyes have ever encountered. Pacing and trying to keep my cool, I waited for over five ours to find out, yes, my mother had survived. Visiting her in ICU was still as hard as ever, but she was home in no time. She had to undergo twenty radiation treatments, also having to shave her head because her hair was falling out. You can't forget something that turns out like this. My mother has always been there for me since my first breath, and I will be there for her until her last. She has been through so much in her life, and she's still standing strong through every single let down. I care about her so much and I have no idea what I'd do without her. God put her on this earth to teach me to stop analyzing the past, stop planning the future, stop trying to figure out precisely how I feel and sometimes to just understand whatever happens, happens. I've been blessed with a wonderful, amazing, and outstanding hero that is one of a kind. Whether our relationship is strained or easy, aggressive or amiable, I will one day need her if only in memory, to remember our history, affirm our femaleness or guide my way. We have our ups and downs, but I would not trade my mother for the world. I'm happy to see my mother is back on her feet and recovering. A guardian angel has been watching over her and my family. Without that angel, my mother wouldn't be here, and I would have never known the great things she has overcome. This is her survival story.

One of a Million
Erica Roberts
Siegel Middle School, Grade 8

"Your great-grandmother would give me one every year for Christmas and they mean the world to me." Perched on the shelf like thousands of soldiers examining their captain, my grandpa's figurines meant the world to him. Every morning at 6 AM, I get out of bed, look at that one-of-a-million figurine that sits on that shelf and think about how much it means to me.

It was Sunday morning when my family lost a loved one. As I was on the plane, on my way to what was once his castle, I reflected on the past, on all the stories I have heard.

Taking that first step into that four-sided house that day was like a baby's first steps. All I could see were the millions of soldiers staring back at me. Eyes forward, everyone holding a countless story, a story that I would not get the pleasure of gathering.

To this very day my dream is to secure just one wish. To hear those stories come out of his mouth would mean the world to me.

The next seven words that hit my eardrum made that day a day I will never forget. "Your grandpa would want you to keep one." Those seven words made my day. As I crept my way over to that shelf, all the stories I heard came to me at once. Gazing upon the shelves, with the many soldiers, I didn't know which one I was going to choose.

That one on the back right corner caught my eye like a diamond in the grass. Standing, head tilted down, holding the little red bird in his right hand was the one that stuck out from all the others.

"I remember when I got this one." Hearing in my head the last story he told me. The story about this one, his favorite one. Hearing his voice in my head is what told me that that was the one, the **one of a million.**

My Brother
Steven Granados
Roy Waldron Elementary School, Grade 4

      A special person in my heart is my twin brother Steve. My brother always takes care of me and plays with me. My brother loves me a lot. I play fist to fist with Steve. We watch TV and play video games together. He is the most awesome brother.

My Love
Achok Alier
Roy Waldron Elementary School, Grade 3

      I love my mom. She is the best. My mom trusts me. She trusts me with the house keys because she knows that I won't lose them, and she also trusts me with the computer. She knows that I do the right things.
      My mom reads me stories when I go to bed. She is a good storyteller. Her stories are the best. I feel closest to my mom when she is reading me a story. Our favorite story to read together is Arthur.
      My mom believes in me. She always cheers me on. She believes in me when I play basketball with my aunt or when we play soccer. She tells me I can do anything I set my mind to do. My mom is the best, and I love her more than anything.

Cancer Survivors
Rebecca Lawless
Rockvale Elementary School, Grade 5

My mom and dad are cancer survivors
No more work for them; they are retired
They've had surgery
My sister, too
Please pray for them, me, and you.

I love them so much; they take care of me
They are amazing as you can see
We love them, me and you
Please help me get through.

For Mom and Dad.

My Brother Nick
Wyatt Parkhurst
Rockvale Elementary School, Grade 5

It's been five months since my brother left to go to his mom's. He did not like our rules, and he moved out. I was devastated. Now I have no reason to get up on Saturday, no reason to come home from school. When I play baseball, I get sad because he inspired me to play. When I play Madden 10, I think of him.

I always was mean to him, but he still loved me. I always wanted to go to Kroger because he works there. He made me want to play sports. He made me want to be the best. He made me me.

Nick would sometimes let me win in football, and sometimes he didn't. We would always have a blast. We would even just play simple games like hide and seek. That's how Nick made a handprint on my heart.

IRAQ
Kayla Forren
Christiana Elementary School, Grade 5

I love my dad
I am not **R**eady for him to leave
He is a h**A**ndprint on my heart
I want him to come home **Q**uickly

Mommy
Asianna Vongvirath
Christiana Elementary School, Grade 3

Makes food
Only has one sister
Makes money when she works
Makes my bed for me
Yawns when she comes home from work

My Family
Tucker McAdoo
Christiana Elementary School, Grade 1

Once upon a time there lived a family. The family loved each other.
Then the family was playing ball. Then it started to rain. The family ran inside. Then they drank hot cocoa. Then they lived happy ever after.

Parents
Brooke Adams
Christiana Elementary School. Grade 5

Do you know that my parents love me? Every night they say it to me. Even if I spend the night somewhere else, they call to tell me good night and that they love me. Then, I tell them I love them too.

Sometimes it feels weird to me because I am eleven years old, and they still say good night to me. I really don't care what people think. I'm pretty sure other kids still say good night to their parents too.

The less time you spend with your parents, the less you know about them. If you think about it, you probably want to know a lot about your family. Your parents aren't always going to be there when you get older. So spend time with them while you can. That is what I am trying to do because when I move out, they are not going to be there to tuck me in. I love my parents, but they won't live with me when I grow up.

All I can tell is that family is important, and you should spend time with them. Make an effort to get to know each other. If you will, they will.

Handprints on My Heart
Lauryn Cole
Christiana Elementary School, Grade 4

Handprints on my heart starts with the things I love that make my heart smile: a hug from my sister with her arms soft, warm like my favorite blanket; a kiss from my mother when she tells me she loves me; my dad who loves me from up above in Heaven.

Handprints on my heart will always be my God who takes care of me and loves me, too – no matter what I do. The love I get from all my family will always be a handprint on my heart.

Handprints on My Heart
Taylor Murphy
Christiana Elementary School, Kindergarten

I love my mom because she gives me hugs.

Handprint on My Heart
Abbey McAdams
Christiana Elementary School, Grade 5

Dear Mother, I love you
Stand right here
When I'm with you I have no fear

Through all the dark nights
And all the sunny days
You have helped me in the most shocking ways

You are at the birthday parties
You give the toast
Thank you, my mom, you are always the best host

You have left a handprint
On my heart
To me that is the very best start

Grandpa and Me
Lane Herman
Christiana Elementary School, Grade 3

      My grandpa is special to me because he helps me when I do not know what to do and I needed help. He helps me when I am sick and well. He encourages me to try new things. He gave me my first Krystal hamburger when I was two. He inspired me to ride a bike and hit a ball. I love my grandpa.

My Mom
Katie Hagar
Central Middle School, Grade 8

You gave me wisdom
Your gave me courage
You gave me love
And a place to call home
You tucked me in and watched me grow
You left a mark
A handprint on my heart

Older Sisters
Victoria Wade
Smyrna High School, Grade 11

When you were just a little girl
I came to your family's world.
A few years later down the road
You went to school
And I was alone.
But still I saw you,
We looked at the clouds in the sky so blue.
The pictures we saw all in our minds
Became our dreams in a few years' time.
A nurse, a mom, a teacher too—
We saw in our minds and our dreams grew,
Middle school came around, new friends with them.
We were still together, always friends
High school next and that was new
New friends, new boys, new trials, too.
Against the odds, we beat them all
'Til the biggest trial of them came to call.
You were leaving and I was not.
Two years time is quite a lot.
Who will you be when you come home?
Not the girl, the best friend I know,
She will be gone, you will grow.
I'm prepared for that now, it took a while,
I'll see you off, and do it with a smile
I'm not glad you're going,
But I'm glad of where you'll go.
The road on this journey will shape you, you know.
The woman you'll become is worth it in the end
Because you are my sister, my hero, my friend.

Because You're Gone
Anais Lopez
Smyrna High School, Grade 11

The house is empty,
The rooms are lifeless,
I yearn to come home
And see you, but
You are no longer
Here.

What used to have color
Is now pitch black.

I feel the world incline
Towards me,
Falling on me,
Because you are gone.

I remember the talks,
The laughs,
The arguments,
The pain and the joy,
But what to do now,
You are gone!

I learn to value everything
In my life now,
Because you never know
When It will be gone.

I await your return,
Will it ever come soon?
I know this is not
Forever, but it's
Taking an eternity
To be the family
We used to be,
When you were here.

I need you in my life
To guide me,
To support me,
To love me,
And to always,
ALWAYS
Be there.

But I'm lost
Right now,
Because you are gone.

But we have faith
That one day we
Will be together again.

And when that day
Comes, there will
Be no other moment in
My life that will
Compare to seeing
You, Mom, again.

I Miss You, Papa
Kristin Bowers
Smyrna High School, Grade 10

I miss your smile every time I would walk through the door.
I miss saying, "I love you!" and you saying, "but I love you more."
I miss saying, "Papa, everything is going to be alright!"
I miss you always saying, "I know, I'll live to be 500, because I'm gonna fight!"
you fought all that pain you felt.
you fought the hurt that life dealt.
you fought just to tell me you loved me one last time.
you found so hard, but I guess it was just time.
time to let go of all that hurt and sorrow.
time to say goodbye to tomorrow.
time to let it all go.
time to end the show.
you're missed for the way you would care.
you're missed by people everywhere.
you're missed for all those good days.
you're missed for your loving ways.
you're missed, mostly by me.
you're missed, because to me you're so much more than just a memory.

My Grandma
Rheannon Hart
Thurman Francis Arts Academy, Grade 2

My grandma is part of my family.
I am glad I have a family that loves me.
My grandma and I cook cakes and treats together.
I like cooking with her.
I also like to spend the night with her.
I love my grandma.

Baby Sister
Lily Springer
Smyrna Primary School, Grade 1

My baby sister is Kylee. She climbs all over me and pulls my hair. Kylee cries when she bumps her head. I kiss her to make it feel better.

My Grandparents
Jace Berry
Smyrna Primary School, Grade 1

My grandparents are amazing people. They are happy and friendly. Some wear glasses and have false teeth. They are great cooks. They snore when they are sleeping, but I love them.

Lee-Lee
Kaleia Branch
Smyrna Primary School, Grade 1

My baby brother is fun and bad. He is two years old and likes to play in the rocks. I like caring for him. He is talking now, and he calls me Lee-Lee.

Bizarre Family

Kaleb Lewis
Thurman Francis Arts Academy, Grade 7

I know of a weird family,
Who's wacky, wild, and crazy
As every family should,
They live in a large home,
As all wish they could.

In this wild family,
There is a little girl.
And although she can be mean,
She acts like a sweet monkey,
Just begging to be seen.

In this wacky family,
Another girl lurks,
Mean as snakes and tough as nails.
She finds her strength in sports,
Where her famous swing never fails.

In this weird family,
There is a strong mother,
Whose kindness knows no limits.
But, she can be a little strict
For she doesn't put up with gimmicks.

In this strange family,
A caring stepfather lives.
And, although he is a good man,
His patience is very thin.
He puts up with as much as he can.

In this bizarre family,
There is a weird boy
Who lives in his own world.
He'd rather be at home,
And he wrote this very poem.

Handprints on my Heart
Alexis Underwood
Stewarts Creek Middle School, Grade 6

They are the ones who touch my heart.
They are the ones who love me with all of their heart.
They are the ones that give me all my needs.
They are the ones who feed and clothe me.
They cure me when I'm hurt,
They put me to bed each night,
They are my parents.

My Parents
Marianna Ford
Stewarts Creek Middle School, Grade 6

Dear Mom and Dad,
     I wanted to thank you for always being there for me. I love you guys so much and will always love you forever. Thank you for teaching me life skills that I will use for the rest of my life. You are amazing and you are the best parents ever.
                                                             Love,
                                                             Marianna
P. S. Thanks!

Marianna Ford • Stewarts Creek Middle School • Grade 6

Handprints on My Heart
Jailyn Hicks
Smyrna Primary School, Grade 1

Dear Mom,
  I love you. You make me laf and cry. It's becos I love you so much! You are owas there for me. You no wust tiet. You chrit me like a good kid. You make shr I git to school on time. Mom, I will owes love you intell the day I diy.

Love,
Jailyn

Handprint on My Heart
Jessica Patel
Christiana Middle School, Grade 8

They say your sibling will always be your best friend
But you, my brother, are so much more
You are flawless in my world, better and above
And thanks to you for opening many a door.

You are a getaway from the real world
An affable, vociferous character, if you will
And it's a phenomenal thing to be on your part
So just know that you have left a handprint on my heart.

You inspire me to think outside the box
Not to mention the times I have come to you seeking advice
You are unique but so hard not to love
Just like a mini-boy angel without wings.

Do not even get me started about the many times we have had together
They range from silly voices to Skittles and Sprite!
Remember the time we climbed up that huge tree?
You are ten times more than a best friend; yes, that is right!

Yes, we have had our ups and downs, and I am sorry for everything
We have come so far from our early start
Look back, smile, and just remember
You have left an everlasting handprint on my heart.

My Sister
Diane Olvera
Christiana Elementary School, Kindergarten

Diane Olvera
My favorite person is sistr.

Chapter Two

I Am Handprints

Bug

Layne Nash
Smyrna Elementary School, Grade 5

I am from the feeling of freshly cut grass and birds chirping all the time.
From the sound of splashing in the pool and the warmth of the furnace on a summer night.

I am from the sound of laughter and the smell of delicious peaches.
From the sound my mother saying, "Never say never" and juicy apples for a midnight snack.

I am from the movie <u>Elmo</u> and my mom reading <u>The Very Hungry Caterpillar</u> to me before I go to sleep.
From my cats rubbing against my legs and the sound of my dad starting the grill for our dinner of juicy steak.

I am from the feeling of warm evenings and the sound of my mom helping us with our homework.
From the pictures of Ruby Falls and the beautiful colors of the sunset on a summer night.

I am from the sound of my sisters playing "Guess Who" and my mom reading to me.
From the sound of my dad's car pulling in the driveway, and the feeling of the warm concrete on our feet when we run to him.

From the Family
Nicholas Ged
Stewarts Creek Elementary School, Grade 5

Based on Where I'm From by George Ella Lyon

I'm from basketball games and straight A's.
I'm from Storm, Odie, and Gulliver;
From pulled-out fiberglass and chewed-up dog toys.
I'm from the ongoing river I know so well,
From the wood crushing the mud.

I'm from Nana and Papa;
From hot wings and the 4-wheeler.
I'm from On Demand and Chester Cheetah,
From Cosco's to the lake,
From worms and rods,
From bass and crappie.

I'm from Me-Ma and cousins next door.
From hide-and-seek and Wii Music.
I'm from tartan and bagpipes.
I'm from injuries and stitches.
I'm from Anna Bell and hamburgers.

I'm from the scrapbook of photos,
From the faces in my dreams.
I'm from the touch of hospitality,
From the family of pride.

I Am From

Hannah Adkins
Kittrell Elementary School, Grade 8

I am from the past,
and the memories yet to come.
I am from cold and shaded days,
and warm days under the sun.

I am from the shadows that danced on the walls
as our laughter and play echoed through the faintly lit halls.

I am from a tight space behind the couch,
my very breath stolen by the tension hanging in the air,
as they stalked through the house searching... searching... searching...
for me.

I am from the dark days.
My life was being controlled by the darkness
that lurked in the empty halls of my heart.
I would tread through each day and wonder
If my life was even worth living,
If my heart was even beating.

I am from tears of the broken-hearted,
as they fell upon the wood and the strings,
my fingers strumming each vibration
that echoed throughout my mind.

I am from new people.
I stood aside and watched them,
and I noticed a difference in them that I know I didn't have.
A difference that I wanted.
A difference that I would get if I pushed without stopping,
If I just gave up one thing for another.

I am from breaking chains.
I gave it all away and breathed in a new life.
I gave away all of the pains of my past.

I am from a new presence of Life
my escape from the cold world,
Where I talk to my daddy,
telling him everything...
and him talking back.
Always.

I am from stepping back into an old world with a new life.
Just beginning to learn, grow, wonder, and wander.

I am from the people with whom I've bonded.
Now they feel like a real family to me.
And together, a family, we are known to be...
On Fire.

I am from hellos and good-byes,
how friends are there one moment,
laughing, smiling.
Sometimes crying,
and the next moment, they've gone away.
Gone on in their lives. But they'll never forget me.
And I'll always remember them.

I am from past memories of brokenness.
But I've been redeemed and my life is new.
"Keep your head up," a close friend said.
They're the few, strong words that still bring me through a lot.

I'm from being on fire for Him.
And whenever someone asks me now... Well...
"I have a heart after God and nothing's going to get in the way of
me chasing after him."

I Am Who I Am
Cameron Boupharath
Brown's Chapel Elementary School, Grade 5

I am who I am because my dad showed me how to play football, and that teaches me how to be a team player.
I am who I am because my family plays board games with me, and that teaches me it's important to spend time with the people you love.
I am who I am because my mom would punish me if I did wrong, and that teaches me not to do it again.
I am who I am because my mom showed me how to wash my clothes, and that teaches me how to be responsible.
I am who I am because my dad put a roof over my head, and that teaches me to appreciate his hard work.

I am a team player.
I know it's important to love.
I am responsible.
I know the difference between right and wrong.
I am appreciative.

I am who I am because of my family.

I Am
Leeah Crenshaw
Blackman Elementary School, Grade 4

I am helpful, patient, and loving.
I wonder what will happen in the future.
I hear people talking sometimes.
I see things like I've seen it before.
I want my old friends to move to Tennessee.

I am helpful, patient, and loving.
I pretend that I'm a famous dancer or rock star.
I believe that you can meet your goals if you work hard at it.
I reach for my goals and always try my hardest at them.
I feel like I say something I shouldn't have.
I worry about what's going to happen in the future.
I cry when I see sad movies.

I am helpful, patient, and loving.
I understand that no one can be perfect but you can be great.
I say that I hope the world will be full of new gadgets in the future.
I dream that I could be a famous dancer.
I hope that I dance at dance schools for a long time.

I am helpful, patient, and loving.

I Am
Autumn Kimble
Blackman Elementary School, Grade 4

I am smart, intelligent, loving, and caring.
I wonder how many fish are in the sea.
I hear the wind whistling.
I see rain falling on cold days.
I want to go and visit my dad and stay in Ohio for one month.
I am smart, intelligent, loving, and caring.
I pretend to be a teacher.
I believe that Jesus is my Savior.
I touch my soft blanket.
I feel happy and excited.
I worry about my great grandpa because he is sick.
I cry because I don't get to see my dad a lot.
I am smart, intelligent, loving, and caring.
I understand that I should respect my sisters.
I say please and thank you.
I dream that there is no cancer in the world.
I hope that I will be a teacher.
I am smart, intelligent, loving, and caring.

I Am
Tiffany Quigley
Blackman Elementary School, Grade 4

I am tiny but smart.
I wonder about my dog at home.
I hear her beautiful bark.
I see her eyes gleaming in the sun.
I want to see her soon.
I am tiny but smart.
I pretend she is right beside me.
I feel her love inside my heart.
I touch her smooth fur.
I worry if she is okay.
I cry if she is hurt.
I am tiny but smart.
I understand nobody cares.
I say she is a living angel.
I dream to be a vet and keep her healthy.
I try to do well in school to see her.
I hope she will be all right.
I am tiny but smart.

I Am

Olivia Weaks
Blackman Elementary School, Grade 4

I am a true person.
I wonder if my dreams, wishes, and thoughts will come true.
I see laughter and joy on people's faces.
I want my life and future to be perfect.
I am a true person.
I pretend things are o.k. when they're not.
I feel a breeze of fresh misty air.
I touch my dreams inside floating in my head.
I worry when things go the wrong way.
I cry when sadness rushes to me.
I am a true person.
I understand things aren't going to go the right way.
I say things aren't going to be the same.
I dream about my life in the future.
I try to help people in every way I can.
I hope for forgiveness and a second chance when I mess up.
I am a true person.

I Am

Elim Jo
Blackman Elementary School, Grade 4

I am kind, gentle, and caring.
I wonder about life.
I hear waves.
I see birds.
I want a cure for cancer.
I am kind, gentle, and caring.
I pretend to be a doctor.
I believe in God.
I touch sand.
I feel soft dirt.
I worry that I will have cancer.
I cry when I miss someone.
I am kind, gentle, and caring.
I understand that people are different.
I say I'm happy.
I dream about heaven.
I hope I can see my friend.
I am kind, gentle, and caring.

I Am

Bailey Peacock
Blackman Elementary School, Grade 4

I am amazing.
I wonder if my dreams will come true.
I hear birds chirping in the heavens.
I see a beautiful future ahead.
I want peace forever.
I am amazing.
I pretend I'm on stage singing.
I feel like a bird soaring in the sky.
I touch my dream.
I worry about people in need.
I cry when the sunlight hits my eyes.
I am amazing.
I understand that we will make mistakes.
I say I believe I can touch people's hearts.
I dream in changing the world.
I am amazing.

Alec

Alec Berkstressor
Barfield Elementary School, Grade 3

Alec
It means nice, helpful, and friendly.
It means number one.
It is like the clear sky.
It is like going to Six Flags.
It is the memory of my mom.
Who taught me to be nice and honest.
My name is Alec.
It means I'm nice and helpful.

Sydney
Sydney Westergard
Barfield Elementary School, Grade 3

Sydney
It means kind, nice, loving,
It is the number 10,
It is like strawberries,
It is like going camping with my family,
It is the memory of my mom,
Who taught me honesty and trust,
My name is Sydney,
It means I believe in working hard
And never giving up.

James
Malachi Jones
John Colemon Elementary School, Grade 5

James
Intelligent, Humorous, Energetic, Exciting
Brother of Malachi, Candace, and Daniel
Who loves making inventions, football on warm days, and playing with close friends.
Who is afraid of death, vicious animals, and killers at night time.
Who wants to see the jungles of Brazil, the palaces of India, and Tokyo, Japan.
Resident of Smyrna, Tennessee
Jones

I Am
Christian Trabal
LaVergne Primary School, Grade 1

I am little and a first grader. I am still a brave kid.

Mirrors
Faith Matherly
Smyrna High School, Grade 12

This mirror I see before me has a reflection I don't want to see.
It's laughing in my face and whatever I do I can't seem to stop it.
Should I walk away or should I stay,
If I walk I will run into other mirrors
But if I stay, do you think it will go away or just keep laughing in my face?
Well, I have decided I think I will just take the chance and stay.

MJ
Emily Joiner
Smyrna Elementary School, Grade 5

I am from Murfreesboro, Tennessee known as the volunteer state and a neighborhood full of laughter.
From a black and white collie mix and an orange and white cat called tiger

I am from a house that has a basketball goal with strings that hang up high and hard bricks that fill scratchy.
From a brick house with a three story playground and a garage filled with toys.

I am from a paperback book that wrinkles when you turn the pages called <u>Diary of a Wimpy Kid.</u>
From funny jokes that makes me laugh.

I am from the smell of juicy noodles that my mom cooks in the kitchen and greasy chicken that I love.
From the concession stand with buttery popcorn and salty sunflower seeds

I am from a bedroom full of color filled with clothes and a comfy futon that I lounge in while I watch <u>iCarly</u> on TV.
From a room that is light blue called whirlpool.

Bee
Emily Nash
Smyrna Elementary School, Grade 5

I am from a quiet little neighborhood and the smell of maple syrup on a sunny day.
From a candle that smells like cinnamon apple to two cats named Tigger and Zoë.

I am from my backyard where I kick a ball and play with my sisters. And a yellow pink sky at sunset, where it's like we dance in the sky.
From hot summer days to winter nights, I always keep my house in sight.

I am from cheesy macaroni and creamy soup with crackers and juicy steak.
From cheesy pizza to spaghetti with meatballs and creamy sauce.

I am from books of <u>The Bernstein Bears</u> to <u>Junie B. Jones</u> and <u>Harry Potter</u>.
From the <u>Boxcar Children</u> to <u>Diary of a Wimpy Kid</u>. I know I will always be a book lover.

I am from a family full of happiness to kind friends and neighbors.
From friends' houses that smell like juicy apples and family members that make me smile.

Buzz
Cade Mills
Smyrna Elementary School, Grade 5

I am from Music City, Tennessee where music soars in everyone and people shine.
From the sound of my brother playing the guitar to my mother singing me to sleep; music is played everywhere.

I am from a tender, loving family and caring neighbors to the sight of people waving and the sound of people laughing.
From a small room in size but big in adventure. To the sound of my television and me playing games, my room is special to me.

I am from a family that goes to church on Sunday and prays for each other.
From everyone singing and dancing all day long with love and joy; everyone loves Sunday.

I am from the smell of sweet, delicious pancakes and crispy, juicy bacon that gets me ready for the day.
From the warmth of the hot and amazing steak at dinnertime that fills me up for weeks.

I am from a radio that has songs that are amazing and touching but also loud.
From either soft or ridged I will always know
I am a music lover.

I Am
Eden Halverson
Thurman Francis Arts Academy, Grade 3

Based on Where I'm From by George Ella Lyon

I'm from practicing "Graduation March" on the piano.
I'm from collecting quarters to filling slots.
I'm from reading <u>Nancy Drew</u> and
        other mysteries.
I'm from singing in the choir and doing "Snow Biz!"
I'm from delicious sausage pizza on Wednesday night.
I'm from helping Mom with the new baby.

I'm from Jean and Rick saying, "Maybe next time, maybe not."
I'm from going to New York and the American Girl hair salon with them.
I'm from wearing Grandma Barbra in my locket.

I'm from Grandma and Grandpa Halverson.
I'm from going to Disneyland with them and
I'm from making potholders.

I'm from Emily and Jared
I'm from French crepes, rice, and beans.
I'm from an editor mom and a religion teacher dad.
I'm from Madeleine, Christian, Monet, and Jacob.
I'm from bugging and sharing with them.
I'm from hugging, laughing, and kissing
        my special family.

Why I'm Me
Nash Binkley
Thurman Francis Arts Academy, Grade 6

Based on Where I'm From by George Ella Lyon

I'm from "Good choices each day keep
    the groundings away."
I'm from the little "t" they call a cross.
I'm from nerfin' the night away but
    still keeping track of time.
I'm from the box they call a Wii
    and the discs they sell separately.

I'm from "Brush your teeth twice a
    day and floss once."
I'm from cucumber and tomato grenades
    we hit the moles with.
I'm from the shots fired in the wars
    Doc was in.

I'm from the familiar aroma of
    chocolate chip cookies.
I'm from cows and barns and
    that ol' garden with the best corn in the world.
I'm from that place they call
    Pleasant View.

I'm from those old scrapbooks,
    thrown together.
I'm from Chucky Cheese and
    chubby cheeks.
I'm from wild foods and spicy snacks—
    leave no rock untasted.
I'm from wonders and wows and
    "How does that work?"
I'm from parents basing their
    lives around me.

That's Me!
Alexis Seilkop
Stewarts Creek Elementary School, Grade 5

Based on Where I'm From by George Ella Lyon

I am from the creek down the road,
      from the infections and cuts,
          from jumping the rocks and swinging on the vine.
I am from poopy patrol and scratches all over.
That's me!

I am from Mimi and Papa,
      Frankie's Fun Park,
          and green bean casserole.
I am from chocolate chip cookies
      (brown, gooey,
          like a piece of heaven.)
I am from "manners" and "Eat your spinach!"
      the two separate houses.
That's me!

I am from Nonnie and Poppa-Pete;
      from the bumper pool games in the basement
      and beating my cousins,
      but also them beating me.
I am from the blue cheese muffins
      and spilling water at McDonald's.
That's me!

I am from the boxes in the attic,
      the tennis rackets and trophies,
      and hard-core matches—
      Uncle Jeff and I—
      loving my family dearly.
That's me!

I Am From
Hunter Ozment
Stewarts Creek Middle School, Grade 6

I am from a nice house and a large yard to play in.
I am from Jesus and the way my family and I worship Him.
I am from Lisa and David.
They both love me lots.
I am from many trips to Gatlinburg.
Our favorite cabin is like a second home.
I am from three brothers and one sister.
They all care about me.
I am from a large family.
I am from an admiring and cherishing family.

I Am From
Kelsey Brown
Siegel High School, Grade 9

I am from different-colored uniforms.
I am from bright-colored cleats.
I am from too many blisters on my toes to count.
I am from a variety of colored, pre-wrapped, electrical tape.
I am from year-round soccer tans.
I am from having a shirt from every tournament I have played in.
I am from playing my sport in 40 degree weather.
I have from stinky shin guards.
I am from being responsible for my position on the team.
I am from showing good sportsmanship on and off the field.
I am from white t-shirts with all kinds of stains.
I am from representing my team with pride and dignity.
I am from a handful of injuries.
I am from blood, sweat, and tears.
I am from ten years of soccer.

I Am
Edwin A. Rodriguez
Roy Waldron Elementary School, Grade 2

I am a boy
I wonder how it is in space
I hear my mom
I see my mom and dad
I am a boy

I pretend I am a car
I feel happy
I touch the gold
I am a boy

I understand I need to do math
I say you are a good boy
I dream for a fish
I try to be good
I hope for ice cream
I am a boy

Steven Roberts • Siegel High School • Grade 12

Who I Am
Kelsey Keith
Christiana Elementary School, Grade 5

Based on Where I'm From by George Ella Lyon

I'm from paper cuts, books, and tears
        and dirt-covered bandages.
From softball with my father
        and jokes during supper.
From encouraging smiles
        and pretty dresses and ribbons.

I'm from Little Debbie cakes
        and fried chicken with pinto beans.
From big round bubbles
        and fishing off the pier.
From "Our Little Angel"
        and stories of the past.

I'm from arguments
        and celebrations.
From pride and military men,
        and deer meat from the hunting.
From "I miss you" and "Be good"
        and rolling in the grass.

I'm from speaking for myself
        and living my dream.
From "Mama, come here"
        and "Daddy, I need help."
I'm from solid gold hearts
        and lessons to guide me through life.

I Am

Jazmyn Carothers
Brown's Chapel Elementary School, Grade 5

I am agreeable, favorable, and entertaining.
I wonder why is the sky blue?
I hear peaceful sounds of nature singing.
I see the world in harmony.
I want everyone to feel content.
I am agreeable, favorable, and entertaining.
I pretend to play things that I want to be when I grow up.
I believe I can reach my goals.
I touch the things in life that matter to me
I feel the happiness inside my bones.
I worry about people that die every day.
I cry when something bad is about to happen.
I am agreeable, favorable, and entertaining.
I understand there are hard times in life that I have to deal with.
I say things that encourage people rather than tear them down.
I dream of the good things in life not the bad.
I hope to always see the good in people.
I am agreeable, favorable, and entertaining.

Chapter Three

Handprints of Memories

I Remember
Arisa Ozaki
Siegel High School, Grade 9

Packing my burdensome backpack
On a sunless Friday morning
I barely had enough time to grab a snack
Because I got distracted by the thundering.

I dashed around the house
Making sure I was protecting everything important
Soon all was as quiet as a mouse
Then came a sudden BOOM
                      CRASH
                                BOOM

I remember
Sprinting around my room
Jumping in horror
When I heard another BOOM

When everything was quiet again, I knew the tornado had passed.

Mississippi
Cassady Compretta
Blackman Middle School, Grade 7

        Have you ever thought of how things used to be?
        But sometimes all that's left are your memories.
    Well, back in Mississippi we had crawfish boils every day,
          playing and getting dirty in the mud and clay.
              Oh, but it's not home to me…
                    Mississippi…

Beauty Masked by Danger
Katie Bentley
Central Middle School, Grade 8

The sand was soft on the bottom of my feet. The sun was emitting a warm sea, swimming around me, touching, settling on my skin. The breeze was like a warm exhale from the ocean before me, it lightly lifted my sun-touched hair off my shoulders. The salty smell of the ocean was mixing with the sweet aroma of the dainty flowers in the grass beyond the sand behind me, making a perfect mix of relaxing scents swarming around me. The ocean was untamed like the birds in the sky soaring above it. The sun's brilliant, luminescent light shown through the ocean, giving its teal surface a radiant turquoise aurora. The beautiful, moss green trees towering behind us swayed with every hint of wind, like angel hair in a breeze. The sky was a deep blue ocean all its own. It was a day with an extraordinary sight. My family buzzed around me, trying to capture the magnificence and indulgence this last day on the beach offered us. The vast waves were almost calling me out to them. Why does the last day have to be the most breathtaking? I walked to the water. The sand was almost white powder; I sank with every footstep. I made it to the cold ocean's edge and took a breath. The sweet scents of the ocean air filled my lungs. I almost didn't want to exhale. A thin layer of water rushed around my feet, moving the sand back and forth. As the water was sucked back into the ocean, I stepped forward. I could feel broken shells under my feet as I descended a little bit deeper into the sea. I kept going till the water was at my waist and I was able to swim. The water circled around me, cold then warm. I felt the mushy wet sand beneath my feet swirl around every time my foot pushed the ocean floor as I swam. The water rose a little every time a wave came. I stayed past the waves just a little. I swam for a while and decided to return to land. I had swum just a few feet, when I saw some of the worried looks on my family's faces. The water started to change course and flow backward, like the water on the shore did. I glanced in the direction the water was retreating. At first all I saw was water filling up into an unknown form. Then, my eyes adjusted. The unknown form was, in fact, a wave, a very large, scary wave. It looked like it belonged in a storm, but it was beautiful. I was either paralyzed by some kind of fear or admiring the dangerous beauty before me. Either way I remained unmoving. Panic didn't strike my body until I felt the drops of water on my face. By then it was too late. A rush of water overtook my body, shoving me down, deeper into the salty ocean. I hit the sea floor; what breath I had was knocked out of me. The water around me moved, swirled, and rushed. It pushed my body in every direction all at once. I was now in a completely different world. I was at the ocean's mercy. I hit the ocean floor again, and then got pushed back. It was like I hit a wall. Maybe it was rock or the ground again. No matter what it was, it made me limp. The water was flowing swiftly around me, keeping me in one place. I lay with my back to a hard object. Its surface was jagged, but with a smooth face. Water started to flow back again, fastening me against the surface. I wanted to breathe, but I had to stop the urge to open my mouth and gasp. I felt the rush of sea water switch back to the opposite direction. My hair flowed in front of my face. For the first time in the past seconds, I opened my eyes to see the deep abyss that had swallowed me as its victim. The sun shown through the water highlighting every movement of the blue liquid around me. The water that should be dark was brilliantly bright, showing shades of cold blues from the sea and warm yellows from the fiery star that lit the sky. Then all I saw was the beautiful bottom of a wave passing above me. It moved with the swirling grace of a dancer. It moved with the strength of a lion, with the swiftness of a cheetah. Every movement made by this one wave was revealed by the sun's illuminating rays. This ocean, this wave moved as if it were untouched time itself. I was scared, but this beauty was comforting. This was true beauty masked by lethal danger, and it somehow gave me hope. I was lying at the bottom of the ocean, losing breath by the second. For some reason the beauty of this one wave gave me hope. I had a life to live and to lead. I had goals, I had plans, and I had wishes and dreams. I had a purpose to fulfill and live. I have a purpose with an outcome of inspiration, understanding, and hope. I was not going to give up and let the life drain out of me in the presence of such ravishing beauty. I let the wave's current take me. I was pulled up into the circular wave and then it pushed me down again. I was closer to shore this time, and the wave's back current wouldn't be able to steal me away again as it did before. I smacked the sand with the force of the crashing wave raining down on me. My body hit the sand with force that felt like I was crashing into concrete. Broken shells lying beneath me, poked and scratched my body. I felt a shell penetrate my left arm, and it stung from the ocean's salt water. Then, all the water retreated back to the abyss from which it had come. I lay there exposed now that the water had left. My hair was wrapped around my face; I couldn't see my surroundings. I gasped for air, letting those relaxing scents breathe into my lungs. Still gasping, I flipped over to where I was facing the ground. I moved my left arm back, the shells scraping and digging into me even more. I pushed up, trying to get strength back or figure out if I even had any. I gasped again as I realized what strength I had was over powered by the stinging of my arm, the pain in my back, and the lack of air I had experienced. My mind was not adjusting to where I was, what happened, or the pain. My thought process was shot. My mind was doing everything but registering my surroundings. Everything around me was blurry. I couldn't hear anything but my gasping breath escaping my throat. I couldn't see anything but the water dripping from my hair and the water washing over the sand and then disappearing. I choked out one more breath and my mind cleared. I heard the sound of feet slapping wet sand. The next thing I knew, I was in someone's arms. I was sitting on the hot sand. I felt it warming me from the outside in. I felt the texture of it and the sand sticking to my wet, cold skin. My head felt like a weight that was latched to my body. I coughed. Then my body gasped for air, throwing me into the upright position. In that moment, I saw the ocean in its perfect light. I saw more than that. I saw that I could have drowned. I saw that I had just found hope in beauty masked by danger. How many times am I going to get that opportunity? How many times are any of us going to get that opportunity? It is to have hope when you are at the bottom of an abyss for whatever reason. I had a reason to let go of that surface and get out of that water. I had the faith to let that wave transport me back to shore. You know we are all going to have to fight at some point. We are all going to have to put faith in something at some time. We are all going to have to sacrifice and lose. We are all going to have to face the storm. Life comes in many different shapes and forms. All life is different, but all life has something in common. All life has a purpose. Some of us find that and some of us get lost along the way, or never find the way. Our purpose gives us power. Not demeaning power to hold over someone but an inner power that helps us get past the battles we must face. Our battles come in many different forms, sometimes even the eyes can't see. Either way we must face that storm. Life is not just surviving. Life is having love, hope, faith, and family worth fighting for. I had a reason to emerge from that sea. I had my future life and the people in it. When I have to cross that bridge, I will make sure I have a reason to make it across. I will make it through my storm. Because I know in my darkest moments, there is light on the other side. I will have things to hope for, to love, and to put faith in. I will build my life on moments of beauty, family, faith, and love. And I will use the painful moments in between to learn from. Life is my learning experience. I will not waste it. My life will mean more, and I will live on in the hearts of my loved ones. Life is unexpected and unexplored like the unpredictable ocean that could have taken my life but gave me so much more. Life is a wave we all have to ride, it goes up and down. It goes through storms. But it is beautiful. It is beautiful. The simple word stands for the strongest of points. Beauty masked by danger that you have to recognize. You have to see the beauty. You have to live for the true beauty and what it means. The opportunity this life has to offer us isn't always going to be recognizable. You have to open your eyes to the possibilities this life and its beauty offers us. You just must.

Handprints on My Heart
Rumbi Tawoneui
Central Middle School, Grade 8

Six years ago I lost my best friend to gang violence. Her name was Kaylen Brise. She was eight years old when she was killed. We were walking home from school. We were laughing and talking when we arrived at my driveway. My mom called me into the house. Kaylen gave me a hug and acted like she was going to die any minute. Once I left, she walked away. Three seconds later gunshots were all I could hear. When I ran outside, I saw Kaylen lying on the ground in a puddle of blood. Bullets were in her head, stomach, and chest. Kaylen was very special to me. She was sweet, loving, and outgoing. It hurt me before, and it hurts me now. I wake up every morning crying, but I know she is in a better place. Her handprint is always on my heart.

Never Let Go
Kayleigh Snyder
Rock Springs Elementary School, Grade 5

"Ding...Ding...Ding!" I heard the bell of the ship's harbor which meant the last ship was less than ten miles out. I was holding my momma's hand so tightly that she was probably losing circulation; however, she didn't say anything. "Swoosh!" I looked, and there coming under the bridge came the ship. "Momma! Look!" She turned her head and looked out. I could tell that she saw the ship because she squeezed my hand more tightly than I had squeezed hers."RRRrrr...Rrrr!" You could see the driver pull the horn. "1..2..3..4." Twenty-two men came off the ship, and when the twenty-third came there was a man with dark brown, short hair, hazel eyes, and a round nose like my momma's. I counted in my head, "1...2...3." When I got to three I ran. He held out his arms, and I ran right into them, making him take a step back. "I'll never ever let go!" I shouted with joy. He grinned. Holding me in one arm he walked over to Momma. When I looked up she was crying. I got a little tingle in my throat. It felt like I was going to cry, too. When Momma got to him, she hugged him, also making him take a step back. We stayed locked for over five minutes. When we looked up almost everyone was gone; however, some were still putting their things in their vehicles. As we turned around to get his luggage out of the ship, it wasn't there. "That's okay, Dad, we'll get you more clothes!" I called. They both smiled.

"Let's go home," Dad said in a calm voice.

Austin Lewis • Siegel High School • Grade 12

Me and My Dad
Mitchell McGuire
Blackman Elementary School, Grade 3

Back in 2008, my dad and I went to Purdue University in Lafayette, Indiana. We went to a game against Penn State. It was the best game ever, except Purdue lost. The seats were wickedly hot. The sun was as hot as a tamale. The stadium was made of brick and looked really nice.

When it was over, we walked around campus and saw almost everything. There was one really big fountain. I decided to play in it. It felt like snow, so I froze up. Then, we went to a bookstore on campus. My dad got me a jersey and a jacket. The jersey number was 21. The player with that number is a tight end.

Purdue's mascot is named Purdue Pete. He is always joking around. Sometimes, he starts making the wave. Sometimes he throws a beach ball into the crowd. Purdue has a train named Boilermaker Express. It is extremely loud, so we have to plug our ears. Purdue's colors are black and gold. They are the best colors ever. Sometimes Purdue has a blackout. You should see the teenagers at a blackout game. They are crazy like a pack of wolves.

Then, it was lunchtime. My dad and I went to Pizza Hut. It was the best lunch ever. After lunch we went to see Purdue's basketball court. It was humongous. Then, we walked by another fountain. It was pretty big. I tested it out to see how cold it was. It gave me a chill, so I decided not to play in it.

My dad and I kept walking. Then, guess what we saw? Boilermaker Express. It was really big like a real train, though it was black and gold. Also, it said Purdue. The driver let me honk the horn. It was really loud! By now it was pretty late. We started our drive home. I told my dad it was the best day ever.

Taking a Picture
Jaden Layne
Blackman Elementary School, Grade 2

Once upon a time I took a picture with my baby brother.
He was so cute! I was happy!
He looked like a cute bunny, and I looked like a bunny too.
That was a good time. I liked that day.
It was on a Friday.
That was my favorite day.
I hope you like this story.

The Ferocious Bull
Miguel Bello
Blackman Elementary School, Grade 3

      The day I was chased by a bull was the worst day of my life! When my dad and I went camping in the woods, there were many trees and bushes by our tent, and a few vines on the trees. In the fall cold nights, we heard many wolves howl at the moon, and many other noises. In the morning, my dad and I made breakfast. We had eggs and bacon. That morning we got into the car. When we drove down the road, we saw a gas station.
      It was white with blue paint. We went in, got some ice, some food, and firewood. Then, when we went back to our campsite, there was a bull by the bathroom! It saw that I was wearing a shirt with red on it. Then, it ran after me! It chased me around and around and around the bathroom. I was running like Indiana Jones when a huge rock was rolling toward him. Eventually, my dad got me out of the way. The guy that owned the campground got the bull and put it where it belonged.
      I said, "Where did that bull come from?"
      They brought us to our campsite and said, "It came from that gate." Though Dad and I had a good time, I never want to go to that campground again.

My Trip to Disneyland
Garrett Stirewalt
Blackman Elementary School, Grade 2

      I went on a trip with my family. We went to Disneyland. We went on a Peter Pan ride. It was very fun. The next day, we went on a haunted house ride. It was the best one yet. I saw Grandpa and Grandma there, too. When the day was over, we went home. We had fun that night!

Parents
Alexis Laye
Central Middle School, Grade 8

                            Our little note to you……….
The decisions we've made are ours to own.
The seeds we've planted are the ones we've sewn
Good or bad they were ours to make; can't steal the smiles or forget the fake
Parents don't have a handbook; neither do we. All we know is what we see……
We try to strive to be the best, we sometimes fall on our faces and forget the rest.
But we do grow and often fast, so please remember my hard times don't last.

Memories
Lin Ni
Central Middle School, Grade 7

Remember those memories of the past,
of those long ago,
Remember the laughter,
the tears,
the fun,
the early mornings,
the late nights,
and everything in between
I had thought everything had just begun
The glow of the morning light,
the dark of the cold nights,
the embers by the fire,
just radiating bright,
Secrets kept,
and lies told,
pulled us apart,
more and more
All that's left is a wisp,
a tiny,
pale,
translucent wisp,
memories
of the past.

Memories
Kristen Marr
Central Middle School, Grade 7

Memories, memories, oh how I love my memories
Memories that keep me safe and act as my light
Memories that haunt and lurk in the night
Memories that shadow me, wherever I do go
Memories that float above and lead me safely home.
Memories that live on, but keep me coming back
Memories that hold me close and safe at night
Memories are even sometimes my worst fright
I hold them close and remember the good times that I've had
And even though they come back, I push away the bad
So listen to me when I say, hold your memories close
They will always be there to comfort you,
When you need them the most.

What Is a Special Time?
Jackson Cole
Central Middle School, Grade 8

What is a special time?
This is a question that we ask,
Especially when it is my prompt,
For to write an essay is my task.
A special time is one that's great,
Like the feeling you get after the last dessert you ate.
Anytime that's special to you,
Was exciting, and now can be remembered, too.
For me, my special time was winning a race,
Crossing the line with sweat on my face.
It was worth it, keeping my pace,
To see afterwards, how I placed.

Saturday Morning
Iris Saunders
Buchanan Elementary School, Grade 8

  The sun sneaked through my window, wrapping my room in a warm glow. Saturday morning, my favorite.
  "Good morning," a whisper hazed through my sleepy ears. Strong arms picked me up and my father carried me to the kitchen. He set me down gently, letting my toes dangle just above the cold linoleum floor. "It's pancake time!"
  I giggled, taking my dad's hand and letting him twirl me round and round. Sonny and Cher played on the radio as we poured, mixed, and sang "I got you, Babe."
  The batter sizzled in the pan, popping and spattering like fireworks. Two, four, six, eight buttermilk dreams cascading onto the platter. We ate like royalty, or so I thought at age seven. When we finished, I felt warm and happy, like a pancake myself.
  "I missed you, Daddy."
  "I missed you, too, Love."

Cooking with My Great-Grandmother
Maiah Case
Barfield Elementary School, Grade 4

I remember one day when I cooked with my great-grandmother. She was the nicest person I have ever met. We would always cook together. We made banana bread, cakes, and cookies together. We have cooked almost everything! I love my great-grandmother and I had a really great time cooking with her.

Christmas
Sam Chappin
McFadden School of Excellence, Kindergarten

I help set up Christmas ornaments on the Christmas tree with my family. Then we made cookies for Santa Claus.

Bailey Hughes • Blackman Elementary School • Grade 1

I Remember

Ellen Williams
LaVergne High School, Grade 12

I remember the smell of pine brush burning,
A sweet, musky smell after they were raked.

I remember the ants biting my skin,
Burning like fire and only saying "Ouch!"

And when I rode too fast on my bike
Away from my uncle and scared him half-to-death.
I got a spanking for that.

I remember the glee I felt when we
Would go to my favorite place,
The animals and rides so wondrous to me.
Timeless memories.

I remember the joy of my parents
When we got to keep my brother for Christmas.

I remember that move from warm to cold.
I missed the warmth and family. New friends.

I remember another move from flat to hills,
From snow to a mixture of all seasons.
More new friends.

I remember my excitement when I got my puppy,
My most prized possession.
My four-legged best friend.

I remember Christmas, warm and bright.
Mexican food on Christmas Eve, The Muppet Christmas Carol.

And when my parents gave the generous tip to our waiter.
I remember the tears in his eyes as he tried to thank us.

I remember my birthday. Sweet 16.
Nothing big or fancy,
But the best my parents could give me.
It was wonderful.

I remember the pain. Betrayed. I had never felt this before.
Arms went numb. Breathing increased. Then darkness.
I didn't know "friends" acted this way.

I remember all of this with joy and sorrow.
But this is what has made me, me.
All chapters in my story. My adventure.
And oh, what a wonderful story it is!

The Big Game
Haylee Ferguson
Lascassas Elementary School, Grade 6

    I threw on my shirt, jumped into my pants, and double-knotted my tennis shoe laces. I put my hair into a ponytail as quickly as possible. I heard from downstairs, "Haylee, hurry up. We have to leave in about two minutes." Right before I walked out of my bedroom door, I looked at myself in the mirror and said, "Today is the big day. It is the day I will stand out." I bolted downstairs as my mom handed me my coat, and I thought to myself, "Today is the championship game."As I thought about this my stomach turned inside out.

    I jogged through the gymnasium door and looked up into the stands. My jaws fell wide-open because I was looking at about two hundred people with smiles on their faces hoping that we would win the game. I went to the locker room where I found the rest of the team. My coach glanced at me with a calm set of eyes, but I knew that she was more nervous than any of the teammates and me. Right before I went to try my best to soothe her, the buzzer sounded, and we went out the locker room door.

    Once we walked out everyone was cheering for us. I didn't know about anyone else, but I was a nervous wreck. We sat down in our seats, as the five starters took their positions. The referee threw the ball up in the air and the game began.

    In the first quarter we were losing by fifteen points. By the second quarter we were trailing by six points. By the third quarter we were losing by four points. By the fourth quarter we were behind by two points. I knew we would win if my coach kept Kelsey Smith in the game. Right as the thought entered my mind, the coach made one of the biggest mistakes of her life. She took Kelsey out and said, "Haylee, you are in the game."

    My heart started to race. I stood up and wobbled out to the gym floor. I was guarding the biggest girl on the other team. My mouth dropped as the referee blew the whistle. I ran, dodging the giant-like girl trying to get the ball. Right as Lauren was about to pass the ball to me, I was on the ground. I stood up as quickly as possible hoping that the referees didn't notice the foul. As sure as my luck, they noticed.

    I walked over to the foul line thinking that if I got both shots I would win the game for the team. My heart pounded so hard that it felt like Bigfoot was running straight at me. Sweat ran down my cheek dropping onto my blue basketball jersey. I stood in terror as I aimed at the basket. The ball flew out of my hand; it went into the hoop with a swoop as I smiled out of the corner of my mouth with about five percent more confidence inside of me than before. I threw the second shot with a little bit more effort. The ball circled around the rim of the basket. My mouth eased open as the ball went into the hoop. My face lit up with a smile. We had won the game.

    The crowd went wild. The team ran up to me with smiles across their faces that were bigger than mine, the coach handed me the trophy, and I held it up with happiness glowing all over me. I did what I thought I would never really be able to do. I stood out from everyone else. I knew that I would never forget that day.

Home Sweet Home
Savannah Berry
Lascassas Elementary School, Grade 5

Home sweet home,
What a beautiful sight.
It'll live with you forever,
All day and night.

The smell of home,
Apple pie.
It smells so good.
You just can't lie.

Mom and Dad
Are all so sweet.
They are there for me
In a heartbeat.

I will leave my home,
I will miss it so much.
I cannot resist,
Because it loves me a bunch.

Preschool Handprints
Aleah Nicholson
Kittrell Elementary School, Grade 4

One day I was in art class. I was four so I was in preschool then. My class and I were making and painting plaster handprints. It was so much fun, but we all got really messy. The next day we got to paint the plaster prints. I painted part of my hand purple and the rest of it pink. The following day was Valentine's Day, so I decided to give it to my dad. I hid it in my room and my dad didn't find it. One hour later, I got it out of my closet and gave it to my dad. He was so happy. Now we can always remember how big my hand was in preschool.

Football
Logan Parker
Eagleville School, Grade 8

It was the last quarter and we were losing forty-six to eighteen with two minutes left. I felt nervous when I heard the coach tell me I was going in the game as tailback. I only knew a few plays and every time I had run the ball before, I had never made it past the line of scrimmage. It was my chance to show everyone what I was made of.

I had been on defense for the past few plays and I deflected a deep pass. They punted to us and we got it on the ten yard line. In the huddle I saw a few of the guys' facial expressions saying, "Oh no, Logan. We have no chance." I was ready to show them wrong. I was definitely the shortest guy on the field and no one thought I could run but coach. The odds were against me.

"Pro-right-twenty-seven." I knew that play. Off we went. I felt the ball being tucked in my arms as I saw a hole forming for me to run through. I ran as fast as I could. Two guys were coming toward me. So, I outran one and the other grabbed the back of my leg but I stayed up. Then, two more came; but I outran them, too. There was only one man between me and the end zone, seventy yards away. He was only a few inches taller than I. So, I hit him as hard as I could and he fell on his back! I was in the open field. I ran faster than I ever had before until someone grabbed my leg and pulled me down on the forty yard line.

I ran two more plays, one for twenty yards and the other thirty. I got a touchdown! I couldn't believe myself, ninety yards in three plays. When we were back on defense they threw a short pass and the receiver was running down the sideline. I tackled him. For my first year playing, I think that I could not have done any better. I will always remember that game.

My Rabbits
Jake Wiebe
Eagleville School, Grade 3

Long ago, I had a rabbit. Her name was Ruby. She had four babies. They stayed in the garage.

Every day I played with them. Playing with rabbits is fun. But not when they are mad. That is just painful.

But one day, I didn't shut the garage door all the way. One, two, three, four, five, they all hopped out.

The next morning, I went outside. I saw a big snake with five humps. I told my dad and he killed the snake. Then we cut the snake open. One, two, three, four, five. The rabbits moved away. It was a miracle!

We took them to the vet. They all were okay but one. The next morning the mamma was dead.

Two years later we had ten more babies. We couldn't take care of all of them so we sold them for $10.00 a piece.

Now I have two cats, two frogs, and three dogs.

I Remember When
Hannah Cron
Eagleville School, Grade 6

I remember when you used to work in the garden all day.
I always went to help you when I came out to play.
I remember when you would fall asleep in your chair.
When I tried to sit with you, you wouldn't move, not even a hair.
I remember when you and Mamaw used to laugh together.
It was always a joyful sound because you wouldn't stop, ever.
I remember when you passed away.
Even though you're gone,
I know you're with me today.
Although we are apart,
All our memories last in my heart.

Dear Mom
Kent Srisavanh
Central Middle School, Grade 8

Dear   Mom,
Hey mama,   I'm writing
a letter to you to let you know
I love you with all of my heart!
You make me smile when
you try to crack a joke.
You are a joy to have
for a mom. You
love me and
I am glad
I'm your
child.
Kent

The Contest
Danielle Driver
Eagleville School, Grade 9

Sitting in the van, listening to my brothers argue, I mutely wrote down random things that came to my mind. It turned into a kind of To Do List: golf, swim, eat out at least once, hunt for crabs, search for seashells, and win the family contest. I had just jotted down the last thing on my list when Eli rudely interrupted me thoughts. "Danielle!"

"What did I do now?" I asked.

"Why did you take the last Jolly Rancher?"

"I didn't know it was the last one."

"Well next time you better give it to me."

"Okay then, Mr. Bossy." I mumbled under my breath. He's only five years old, so he believes that the world revolves around him. I usually just have to go along with his ornery, whiney attitude, because my mom and dad always say, "It's a phase. He will grow out of it." Well, sometimes it seems like he's taking to long to grow out of it.

After a long, aggravating car ride, my family had finally reached our destination, a beautiful hotel named Caribbean. The whole building was constructed of red-colored bricks, except for the occasional tan-colored brick, here and there. When I stepped out of the van, I noticed that all of the tan-colored bricks actually formed a big "C," which had to stand for Caribbean. I thought that was really creative. The rooms of the hotel were also beautiful, and very well equipped. Our room included a kitchen, two bedrooms, a sunroom, and two bathrooms. The whole place felt so cozy and comfortable, like as if we were meant to stay there. This was by far the nicest, and coziest hotel I had ever seen.

After we had finished the thrilling, exciting job of unpacking, my parents sat my brothers and me down on the brown leather couch in the living room. We always went through this same procedure on every trip, so I knew we were going to discuss the family contest. Every trip that we take, we always come up with a contest, and whomever wins the contest receives a prize. This year we had to try and find the most beautiful seashell, or the "coolest shell" as my brothers put it. I didn't think this would be hard at all. I could, and would win this easy contest.

Once we finished talking, we hopped into our car and drove towards the putt-putt golf course. When we arrived, we paid for everybody, picked up our putters and golf balls, and walked to hole number one. Daddy decided to go first, so he automatically dropped his ball on the green. He then took a couple of practice swings to judge how hard he needed to hit the ball. I wanted to say that this wasn't a real golf course, and the score didn't really matter, but I thought it would be best if I just kept my mouth shut. Finally, after what seemed like forever, he tapped the ball, and then everybody fell silent. Eli didn't even say a word. The ball was heading straight towards the hole. Was he actually going to get a hole in one on the first hole? Then, the ball started to roll along the edge of the hole, and lucky for him, it plopped right in. "Lucky." I said.

"No, that was skill." my dad replied.

"Sure. Sure."

The rest of the game was pretty relaxed, except for the occasional hole in one, here and there. Then, at the eighteenth hole, Daddy and I were tied at a score of forty-five, and we were both on our last putt. If my ball went into the hole and Daddy's didn't, I would win the game! On the other hand, if my ball didn't plop in and Daddy's did, I would lose, again. The game was on the line. It was my go first. I swung my putter and hit my lucky purple ball. It rolled and rolled around the rim, and then it dropped right in! "Yes!" I yelled. "Your turn." Daddy looked at me out of the corner of his eye, and then started his practice swings. After his third practice swing, he decided that it was time to hit the ball. He swung his putter and his ball started rolling towards the hole. It rolled around the edge of the hole, just like mine had, but instead of dropping in, it decided to stay on the green! He had missed his shot, which meant that I had won the game! This week was actually starting off very well, for me at least.

The rest of the week was very relaxed and I had completed almost everything on my list. On Tuesday we went crab hunting. Wednesday we went swimming and golfing. And Thursday we went out to eat at TGI Friday's. By Friday though, I still hadn't found the perfect shell. How was I supposed to win the contest if I didn't even have one shell to show? I had thought about the seashell the entire trip, even when I was golfing or swimming, but there never seemed to be enough time to go seashell hunting. Today was going to be different though. "Mom, can I ask you question?"

"I'm in the kitchen!" she answered. I strolled into the kitchen and plopped down on a stool.

"Since everybody else is asleep, could you and I take a walk down to the beach?" I asked.

"Sure, just give me five minutes." Once she finished what she was doing, we strolled down to the beach together. I now had a mission. I was going to uncover the most beautiful shell in the world. As soon as my feet hit the sand, I started searching, but even after about twenty minutes, I was still left empty-handed. What was I going to do? Then, my mom called out to me, "Time to go!" She had already started heading back, so I mutely dragged my feet towards the hotel.

"Ow!" I screamed. "What was that?" I lifted up my barefoot and underneath it there was a pointy object sticking up out of the ground. I dug it up and to my surprise it was, or what looked like, an old hermit crab's home. It had brown swirls running all the way around it, and little brown polka-dots spread randomly all over it. There was no doubt in my mind that this shell could and would win the contest for me.

"What is taking you so long?" Mommy asked me.

"Oh, nothing." I answered cheerfully.

"Well then, come on. The boys are probably wondering where we are."

"Ok!" And with that, I picked up the seashell, placed it in my pocket for safe keeping, and then skipped the whole way back to the hotel.

When we returned, I was so excited that I couldn't wait until the boys woke up. How could they sleep so long? We had been gone for thirty minutes, and they had already fallen asleep an hour before we left. They must have been really tired. The boys finally started waking up one by one. Daddy came first, then Austin, and eventually Eli and Levi exited their room. It was now time for the contest I had been waiting so long for. We all gathered around the coffee table and took turns displaying our shells. Daddy, of course, went first and displayed his shell for all of us to see. It was a tan colored shell with sharp little ridges running down it. Then, Mommy showed off hers, and it was a little, tiny shell with a natural hole carved into it, which she was going to use to create a necklace. My three brothers, also, had found shells, and they showed us three pretty little white shells. The shells were almost identical. After my brothers presented their shells, they had to take time to explain to my parents that they absolutely had to win. I don't remember their exact reasons, but I think they just wanted to have a chance to brag about something, and to make everybody's life miserable. I was the last to show my shell, but everybody still loved it. They all wanted to touch it, and hold it, and even try to hear the ocean's song in it. I was very happy.

It was now time to vote on who had discovered the best shell. Was it going to be me? I sat there, tensely, throughout the voting process. I couldn't vote for myself, because that would seem selfish, so I raised my hand for Mommy's shell. When my dad finally asked for votes for my shell, everybody raised his hand! I was so excited that I almost forgot about the prize. After I calmed down a little, my dad handed me my very own scrapbook! It was painted a beautiful teal color, and it was decorated with pretty little flowers and stars. It was one of the best gifts that I had ever received.

At the end of the day, when I was climbing in the van for the trip back home, I started thinking about my day. I had received two wonderful items in just one day, a seashell and a brand new scrapbook. Amazing!

Footprints in the Sand
Michaela Marcum
Rock Springs Middle School, Grade 7

Every night I lie awake
With the memories that haven't yet faded
From the one or two summers
With all of my friends.
We'd watch and play volleyball
Our feet in the sand.

We swam every Thursday
And made jokes by the tree.
We lay on our hill
My sis, our friends and me

I remember watching clouds roll by,
While singing my favorite song
And time came for me to go.
I still can't move on

Now every year as time marches on
I hope to go to the beach
Where I swim and construct sand castles
Leaving footprints in the sand

Graveyard Hunting
Emily Sellers
Riverdale High School, Grade 11

We begin our journey in an Oldsmobile—yellow.
Elton John plays softly, familiar and mellow.
As the top is let down and the breeze let in,
The afternoon sun warms my childish grin.

I look at Dad, he's trying to get lost,
And I hope our paths cross.
I adjust myself on my tall booster seat
(It's the only way the road and my eyes can meet.)

As the old country roads twist and twine,
We finally spot a graveyard's ancient outline.
I jump out of the car, not the least bit afraid,
And begin to examine the history, decayed.

I look at the beds of those long passed,
Hoping they don't mind that I've trespassed.
Some are crumbling and old, some are new,
All displaying messages of final adieu.

I can feel the love and see the time,
While the trees breathe whispers benign.
All too soon the sun starts to set,
And we depart against my requests.

I am once again placed atop my plateau.
As my adventure and eyes come to a close,
I dream of places unexplored today,
But I'm here with my dad, and that's okay.

Ode to Jeffery
Kirstin Williams
Riverdale High School, Grade 12

My father's job once again was relocated
And no matter how much I complained and debated
My parents said we were to move a fifth time
From Utah we would cross the Tennessee line
All alone and without any friends or hope
Crying myself to sleep was how I would cope

My parents wanted me to be happy once again
So they decided to let me have a little friend
They took me to a small farm to buy a pet
And once I saw her, my mind was set
She was the cutest goat in the entire world
I named her Jeffery even though she was a girl

Finally, I had my first friend in Tennessee
And even as strange as it may be
I now had a reason to enjoy my life
But then something happened that stabbed me like a knife
Little did I know that my happiness would end
When a dog attacked my only friend

I got home from school and my dad knelt down
He sighed and then said with a frown
A dog had jumped the fence and then I could tell
That the end of this story would not end well
The only reason keeping me going was no longer here
So once again I disappeared

Going to Disney World
Carson Boyd
Wilson Elementary School, Grade 1

My favorite vacation was when we went to Disney World. It was cool meeting the characters and going on the riders. Space Mountain was great! I can't wait to go back.

The Little Girl in the Big Woods
Chloe Ownby
Wilson Elementary School, Grade 1

I like to go to MaMaw and PaPaw's house. They live on a hill in the woods. They have a lot of big trees. I can pretend that I am in the forest. I have to build a fort out of sticks. If I don't, the bears and snakes might eat me! I better run inside and have some hot cocoa instead.

Fall Fun
Kendall Miller
Wilson Elementary School, Kindergarten

My dad and my sister and I jumped in the leaves and made patterns with the leaves. We made a big pile of leaves for my dad to jump in.

A Day at the Beach
Jordan Watkins
Wilson Elementary School, Kindergarten

We went to Florida. We got on a canoe boat. We went out into the ocean. We saw dolphins. We got out of the boat and swam in the ocean. We saw sharks after we got back in the boat. I nearly drowned when a big wave hit me. We picked up seashells on the beach. Then we went back to our hotel.

Nonnie's Camping Trip
Riley Carter
Wilson Elementary School, Grade 1

This summer I went camping with Nonnie and Don. My cousins went, too. We roasted marshmallows and sang campfire songs. I slept on the top bunk in the camper. I can't wait to go again.

We Went to the Fair!
Morgan Reasonover
Wilson Elementary School, Grade 1

I love my whole family. We went to the county fair. We stayed at a hotel. I rode a horse named Peanut. We had a lot of fun at the fair.

My Dog
Devron Burks
Wilson Elementary School, Grade 2

      I always wanted a dog. We were at my aunt's house one night making smores when a dog suddenly came out of nowhere. My brother and I asked if we could take him home, but my mom had to check the neighborhood to make sure he didn't belong to anyone. The next morning my mom found out that he didn't belong to anyone so we poked out our lips, put on our saddest faces, and hoped that our dad would say we could take him home. He finally said yes and we were so excited! We picked the name Midnight since he came to us at nighttime and he is black. Once we got him home he began to chew everything in sight, so we quickly changed his name to Chewy Midnight Burks. My brother and I are still very happy to have our dog!

My Trip
Savannah Bowen
Walter Hill Elementary School, Grade 2

I loved the day Mom, Dad, and I went to Disney World. We rode lots of rides and spent lots of time together. I loved spending all that time with my parents. I love them very much.

Swimming with the Wild
Sydney Russom
Siegel Middle School, Grade 8

One of the most exquisite events to take part in is swimming with dolphins. Most people swim with trained ones; however, I got the ultimate experience of swimming with the one hundred percent pure wild beasts.

It was August of 2009, my spunky family and I were on vacation at the lovely Seacrest Beach where we settled in a three-story beach house (that even came equipped with a golf cart) in the gated community of Pelican Manor. As I pulled myself out of bed one morning I quietly suggested, "We should make our jet-skis useful and go jet-skiing in the ocean." Next thing I know, I'm cruising on the highway towards the bay.

We arrived at the small bay of Seacrest Beach and unloaded our jet-skis for an unforgettable journey. Boy, was the water beautiful out there! The luscious shades of baby blue and turquoise stuck out like a sore thumb in the endless miles of sand like finely grained woodchips. The water was so transparent, you could see clear to the ocean floor where clans of joyful jellyfish jumped around. Suddenly, I saw some dorsal fins off to the right and immediately thought shark, but as I studied the creature I realized it was a cute, little dolphin! Actually, the dolphin was quite large. Some looked seven to eight feet long!

Finally, after minutes of my dad teasing me to jump off, I built up the courage to jump into the friendly waters. As I inched closer to the amazing creatures, I noticed their damaged fins and for the first time I really appreciated what these dolphins stood for. These majestic animals strive for excellence and companionship. They always travel in groups to be there for each other in times of peril. Dolphins are really what we humans should be like. We humans should stick together and become allies with each other. Dolphins are true role models to the human race and I am ecstatic to have been so close to some true heroes.

Memories
Noelle Henson
Siegel High School, Grade 10

At the foot of the bed in the cedar chest,
Spilling with old photos, letters, mementos,
A remembrance of what has been and done,
And a semblance of actions in memory.
I am from these moments.
Molding me, making me,
Who I am.

Lean Levis and backyard bonfires,
Adding to the awe of never ending nights.
The aroma of lush lawn and grandmother's gingerbread,
Shaping a soulful summer into a winter wonderland.

From mis amigos and l'amoir de ma famille.
Creating the magic of Cinderella
And red-haired adventures under the sea.
The influence of He who is holy,
The gossips and secrets.
The teethless gums of my grandfather,
And the scar of mystery on my grandmother's knee.
These precious memories paint me.

At the foot of the bed in the cedar chest
Filling with new photos, letters, mementos.
A remembrance of what is being done,
Semblance of actions fresh in mind.
I am from these moments.
Transforming me, creating me
The one I am soon to be.

My Vibraphone
Keaton Davis
Siegel High School, Grade 10

Instead of going home and burning the house down after school, I spend every week, Monday through Saturday, with the marching band. As a member of the frontline, I play the mallet instruments in front of the band. Go figure. We are also known as "the pit," a rather unfortunate name that has been bestowed upon us by someone mean. I like to go by the name "frontline," which sounds a lot more impressive, and doesn't involve the underarm.

The most amazing experiences I have in the band are at the competitions we go to nearly every Saturday during marching season (better known as football season). The Contest of Champions at MTSU last year was the most exciting contest we went to out of the four that season. My stomach was a like churning sea during a storm as the frontline walked out onto the bright green turf, clad in our navy blue and teal uniforms, our black-shoed feet bouncing off the springy ground. The Pit Packers, the fathers who help us move all the equipment from place to place, were in stride with us. I looked up at the stands, a gigantic mass of wriggling specks in the shadow of the afternoon sun glaring in our eyes.

We had very little time to get everything into position. The xylophone in the center, with the bells on its left, followed by two vibraphones. The two wooden marimbas resided on the xylophone's right. I played the whole show on the last vibe, the one that had been found as a pile of bars and wood one day and rebuilt by one of the band dads into what the frontline now calls "the ghetto vibe." I like it a lot, though, despite what everyone says about its scratched silver metal bars and its old black frame. Although some of the natural wood shows in the form of thin gashes from who-knows-what, it still serves its purpose. The pedal that is used to remove the dampeners from the bars, causing them to ring like beautiful bells on a clear night, creaks, and is hard to push down. Everything about it seems raggedy, like a teddy bear that has been hugged and drooled on for days at a time and washed several times after being dropped in the toilet. It is very worn and used looking, but it is important and valuable, at least to me. It still makes beautiful sounds, however, when I play it with the green yarn mallets, and that's all that matters.

At the contest, I got in position behind my vibraphone, my baby, and looked in towards the xylophone at my section leader, Mary. Megan, the drum major, started conducting, and the whole frontline began to pulse our mallets to the beat, locking in with one another. Mary and the two marimbas next to her played straight eighth notes, while Robert, my vibe buddy, and I played syncopated rhythms. Then the rest of the band came in, and we played what was going to be our best show of the year, and it should have been; it was the last competition of the season!

While I played, all the emotions that had bottled up inside of me over the previous days all leading up to the moment we stepped onto the green field began to burst out of me as I played, like lava erupting out of a large volcano. All the anger, frustration, and every other intense feelings that were inside me escaped, just like they fled every other band member on the field. They came out in the form of notes, rhythms, and chords that permeated the stadium, filling the audience with a mixture of awe and excitement. When we came to the ballad, the slow part of the show, our emotions receded from intense and aggressive to calm and flowing, matching the smooth sounds coming from the band.

Then those emotions built up again as we played our percussion feature, the frontline's and the drumline's chance to shine. The frontline played a long, intense run, to which the drum answered back with a nice lick on the snares, tenors, and basses. Our conversation continued until the band returned with the closer, and we built up all the remaining power and intensity to blast away the last note, causing the whole stadium to erupt into applause and a standing ovation. As we marched off the field, the Pit Packers following closely behind, I thought to myself, "This is only preliminaries! One more show to go for tonight!" The adrenaline that was pumping through everyone else's body kept us energetic until finals that night. We played our show with even more intensity than before and blew every other band off the field.

A while later as our band stood at attention on the field amidst the other eight bands that made it to finals, we found out that we made Reserve Grand Champion, and John Overton High School got Grand Champion. We were overjoyed that we had made such an amazing achievement! That shabby vibraphone had got me to where I was, a very excited, proud member of the Siegel High School Marching Band. It is still my baby, even this year. Although I don't play the vibe at all for this year's show, which, by the way, is ten times better than last year's, the new freshmen are able to experience its magic, and understand what they can do to make it truly shine, not in appearance, but in musicality.

That vibe has just as much power and intensity as the player puts into it. It doesn't matter what it looks like. It is the vessel of our emotion and in using it, we form that emotion into beautiful, overwhelming, flowing sound that creates a new world for the audience to enjoy.

Burning down my house, or creating wonderful music...I choose my vibe.

Reflections of Joy

Amy St. John
Siegel High School, Grade 11

Love, life, and laughter
Where to begin?
There aren't words to describe all of my happy memories
Shared with family and friends
All of the crazy tales and wild adventures of years past
A picture is worth a thousand words, you say?
Not even a picture could sum up everything
Snowball fights, lemonade stands, and carving pumpkins
Splatter paint parties and movie-watching, riding bikes
Watermelons, and water balloons, s'mores, and inner-tubing,
Climbing trees, and swimming pools, chasing down the ice-cream man
Shopping, talking, trick-or-treating, yelling, singing, laughing
Interesting how,
the smallest things in life
leave the largest handprints on my heart

Kylea Carver • Thurman Francis Arts Academy • Grade 6

Tara

Emily Duchac
Siegel High School, Grade 11

I love... friends. Animals. People. I love... running. Reading. Writing. Drawing. Painting. But most of all, I love... dancing. And that passion has changed my life in more ways than one. Sometimes, the change came from inside, came from me. But more often than not, that change came from outside, from someone else. From a teacher, a friend, a confidante. And one person to fit that description is one of my very first dance teachers, Tara.

Tara was my idol. She only taught me for a year, but she was eighteen, and she was beautiful inside and out. She was an amazing dancer, an expert in every field, but most skilled in mime, contemporary. And she was invincible. Or so I thought. How could someone like Tara not last forever?

I was five or perhaps six. Every day, I'd come to the studio for an hour or two or three and Tara would teach me. Sometimes I'd go to a class, but usually I took private lessons. We'd dance for a while, talk for a while, dance a little more. For an entire year, this routine happened without fail. Then, one day I showed up at the studio and Tara was in jeans. And she was sitting down, heavy bags under her eyes, looking even skinnier than usual. I almost didn't recognize her; I'd never seen her out of tights.

Tears in her eyes, Tara proceeded to tell me that she was moving to Wisconsin and that I might not ever see her again. I burst into tears. What was I going to do without Tara? I missed her already. Her dad came into the room, helping her to lead me back to the car. Wrapping me up in a hug, Tara whispered into my ear, "I love you, Emily. And I'll miss you. But you have a wonderful future ahead of you." Sniffling, I finished my goodbyes and went home.

Several years later, I was looking through some old papers when I came across a newspaper clipping. I was about to throw it away when I noticed a picture of my old dance teacher Tara. It was a short obituary. She had passed away at the ripe old age of nineteen from cancer. She had quit school to teach dance full time when she found out that she wasn't going to make it.

The news hit me hard. I wasn't sure what to think, how to feel. Tara, my Tara, was dead. Had been dead. After the shock passed away, I realized what an inspiration my teacher was. She could've just given up on life, sat at home, and withered away. Instead, she chose to spend her time teaching children, and more than just dance. She taught me how to live my life, how to set my priorities straight. And she taught everyone she met how to shine, how to keep going when all hope was lost. Tara was everything that I strive to be.

The Once a Year Trip

Jenny Newman
Siegel Middle School, Grade 6

It was a bleak, cool winter day. The air was crisp with a scent of pinecones. I was on a trip to East Tennessee, something I look forward to all year. Sometimes we are able to see the amazing snow-capped Smokey Mountains. This story takes place on a hill in a little town called Morristown.

On that hill, there is an early Christmas celebration with family from near and far. It happens once a year; we all gather and have so much fun. I like it because I get to play with my cousins and see all the rest of my family that I normally don't get to see a lot. I usually get to spend the day with my mamaw before the celebration. It's so much fun! The scenery on the way to my Aunt Elsie and Uncle Ronnie's house is very beautiful inside; their house is phenomenally decorated.

The main thing that makes the trip worth waiting for is seeing the family and giving them presents. The cool thing about this is getting to see the looks on their faces when they open their gifts. One cool thing that my cousins Caroline and Wesley and I get to do is to help with passing out all of the presents. We are kind of like Santa's helpers!

Christmas dinner is usually served before presents, and it is a treat! The food is amazing. The scent of it has melt-in-your-mouth all over it. One little secret – Aunt Elsie always makes my favorite, deviled eggs. She is a master cook. Afterwards, we usually have a fabulous dessert.

I'm pretty sure by now you can understand why I love Christmastime and going to East Tennessee. It's not because of the presents. The truth is I love it because I get to see all of my loving family!

The China Rabbit
Natalie Palmer
Siegel Middle School, Grade 8

There once was a pink rabbit with soft ears, lace around its hands, and four bows, two for his feet and two buttoning up his outfit. It sat upright in a small toy store with other baby toys. Late in the afternoon with the sun like a king high in the sky, a woman with curly black hair picked it up, thinking it would be perfect for her new baby.

No, the woman wasn't pregnant; she was going to adopt a beautiful new baby girl from Chongqing, China. Her husband came along with his bright blue eyes and agreed it would be perfect. Little did the rabbit know that he was going along, too!

No sooner had the rabbit been bought than they packed and started soaring to Hong Kong, China. The rabbit could not see much, being stuffed into a bag that was blacker than a witch's cauldron. Not only that, he was piled in with Nora Roberts books, clothes, and other various traveling necessities. As soon as the plane lifted off, the rabbit clunked into a hard book below. The rabbit never saw out the window the cool, captivating scenes of Connecticut or beautiful Boston, but he did hear people laughing, snoring, and talking along the way.

Finally, the long journey was over. When the bus drove to the couple's hotel the rabbit could hear the hustle and bustle of people in the streets and a difficult foreign language. After the couple got to the hotel, the rest was a blur, for the rabbit was stuffed back in that black cave for days! Eventually, it got picked up and driven to a huge building with kudzu creeping up the sides. The waiting took forever for the rabbit, but the babies eventually began coming out with their nannies.

The couple got their baby and tears streamed down. There she was all bundled up with her face barely showing. The first toy they showed her was the pink rabbit, and she loved it. Later, she slept with it in her soft crib.

If you are wondering how I know all of this, it's because it was my adoption and my story. Hop-Hop, the rabbit's name, is still with me today in my extremely messy bed. He travels with me and goes wherever I go. He always has listening ears and attentive eyes. Hop-Hop the rabbit was my first toy, first friend, and first treasure.

Just Like Me
Caitlin Meier
Siegel Middle School, Grade 8

      As I walked into my dance studio a little early for my afternoon rehearsal that summer day, I saw a giddy little girl, all ready for ballet class. Her name is Ella, as I now know, and she was wearing little pink tights, a black leotard, pink silk ballet slippers, a purple ribbon tying her blonde curly ringlets at the top of her head, and her pale pink Hello Kitty dance bag all ready for her first day of ballet. I could see her excitement, and some of her nervous jitters just waiting to burst out like a firecracker exploding into the sky.

      Watching this little girl brought back so many memories for me that day. I remembered when it was my big day, and I sat watching in awe the big girls who could stand on their tippy toes as they laced up their satin pointe shoes and wrapped their hair in a tight bun. I thought of how I felt when they asked me if I was excited, and how I so badly wished I could be just like them. The memories of seeing them do their perfect turns all the way across the dance floor and leaping as high as the sky all came flooding back to me like a burst of wind knocking me off my feet.

      While preparing myself for rehearsal to begin, I talked to Ella, asking her questions. "How old are you? Is this your first day?" …small talk. I learned that she was four years old, and that "today was ballet day," as she told me. She told me how her mom took her to pick out her tights and leotard after preschool yesterday and that she was so excited!

      As the clock kept ticking, time for my class grew nearer and nearer. I took off my street shoes and warm-up set, and began to tie up my new pointe shoes. I combed my hair, and just like I had seen those big girls do, I wrapped my hair in a tight bun. Finally four-thirty arrived, and as I walked into class, Ella said, " I want to be just like you!"

      Looking back, I realize that I was once that giddy little girl waiting for the first day of ballet class. I once looked up to those big girls who could stand on their tippy toes. I wanted to be just like them! I also realize that now I am one of the big girls who can leap as high as the sky. And I have little girls, like Ella, who want to be just like me. I will hold on to this memory forever, like a "handprint on my heart."

Christmastime
Yuleni Cardenas
Roy Waldron Elementary School, Grade 4

      A special time for me is Christmastime. Christmas is a great time for my family. During Christmas, I get a lot of presents. My grandmom makes delicious food. Family members come to visit, and we have a great time. Christmas is nice because everybody puts Christmas trees in their houses, and they put lights on the outside. Christmas is the coolest holiday.

When I Was Little
Adam Close
Christiana Elementary School, Grade 4

When I was little, my family and I went to a hotel in Gatlinburg. My dad and I were jumping back and forth on the beds. We heard a crack! The loud noise made the people below us very mad. The manager came to our room. He was also very made at us.

My dad had to pay for the broken bed. The next day he said, "Next time we won't do that." I thought it was funny that HE broke the bed!

The Time I Went to Florida
Kaylee Phifer
Christiana Elementary School, Grade 4

The one time I went to Florida I had a great adventure. My Aunt Betty lives in Florida. We went to see her. It was my first time seeing my aunt, so I didn't know her. She is my dad's aunt so she is my great aunt. We stayed there for three days. When it was time to go, I cried, because she was really nice and we had had fun.

When we left Aunt Betty's house, we went to Kennedy Space Center. It was fun. We saw rockets and planes. We also saw alligators. We went to several buildings with displays. We also went to this building where you could watch videos. After we left Kennedy Space Center, we went to our hotel. We settled in and called it a day.

The next day we went to the lighthouse in St. Augustine. The first time I went up there, I didn't go all the way up because I was scared. We went to the gift shop. I got a bell and a teddy bear. I tried to climb the lighthouse again. I went up to the top two times. When we left, we went to the beach. We went back to the hotel to get some rest.

The next day, we went back to St. Augustine. We went on a cruise while we were there, and then we went back to the beach. We went back to the hotel and went to sleep.

The next morning we packed our things and headed home. It took us nine hours to get home. I will treasure this adventure with my family. It was a handprint on my heart.

How I Lost My First Tooth
Shayla Mayo
Christiana Elementary School, Grade 1

When I was six my tooth started to get loose. I was excited that my tooth was going to fall out. My tooth got looser and looser. I could not stop wiggling it. It took a long time to come out.

Soon more of my teeth started getting loose. Finally, my first tooth came out at school. I was wiggling it and wiggling it and I could move it side to side with my tongue. I wiggled it one more time and my tooth came loose and I spit it out on to the table. That's how I lost my first tooth.

We Go Camping
Michael Lahue
Christiana Elementary School, Grade 1

      Daddy loads the van with camping stuff. We drive to the campground. When we get there, we set the tents up, cut wood, and build a fire. We cook dinner and then roast marshmallows. After dinner, we get our sleeping bags ready and go to sleep.
      The next morning, we get up and go fishing. After fishing, we come back to the campground, pack up, and load the van. On the way home, we stop at McDonald's, get breakfast, and then go home.

First Day of High School
Bailee Dover
Smyrna High School, Grade 10

      My first day of high school was a life-changing experience. I remember being so scared, worried, and unsure of just about everything. The drop off for my day to begin was the worst.
      "Go on, time to head out," my mom said with this serious yet sad face.
      "No ma'am," was my reply, with the biggest baby brown eyes, filled with tears.
      "You're going to make me cry. I'm sorry, but, Honey, you've got to get out and go to school," she said as she literally pushed me out of the car and then drove away.
      Once I got of the car and walked in the doors, I was frozen in fear. I could feel the sweat running down my face. I could feel the cold chills appearing on my arms. My legs and hands were shaking violently. I was incapable of moving my legs to walk. Then, my feet began to move slowly. My eyes wandered all around, seeing new faces, new behaviors, and a whole new routine. My fear held my head down and kept my eyes on the floor. I walked down the hallway swiftly and fearfully. Touching people, looking at people, and getting in their way scared me. I did not want to upset anyone today.
      Then I had to go to my classes. My ears heard the bell, but my head heard the screaming of tortured individuals. I made my way to my classes unsure of what to expect. My teachers, my peers, my friends were a whole new adventure. I did not know what to expect, what to say, or what to do. I wanted to make a fantastic first impression. This thought of me will last the next four years of my life! Scary!
      Then when lunch came, oh my goodness. This was also a new experience for me. I walked into the cafeteria and I felt I was looking into a never-ending cave. This place was huge! Where do I go? Where do I sit? What do I do? This time I felt sick to my stomach. I felt all the color in my face just disappear. Luckily, I found some familiar faces and I sat with them. "Whew!"
      This whole new experience was life-changing for me. I became bolder. I now walk down the halls with confidence. If I do not know someone, I take a step and talk to them. Before, I would just sit in the corner and not move. However, I still have the fear of making the wrong impression with people, but over time that will hopefully decrease. I now am a sophomore, and I made it through my freshman year all right! High school is a great place to grow up!

The Fight
Vince Phillips
Smyrna High School, Grade 11

I haven't been in a lot of fights in my life span, although I will admit to a few. The one fight that stands out to me was the one I got into with a girl. This experience truly changed my outlook.

This incident took place in the fourth grade. You see, I was not fully informed on how males were supposed to treat females. I always treated guys and girls the exact same way. After this incident, I quickly realized the difference between the two.

One day a couple of my classmates and I were wrestling outside after lunch during recess. This was a daily occurrence for us. We looked forward to recess just so we could wrestle. This particular day was different than normal. On this day a girl wanted to mess around with us, too. I took it upon myself to initiate her by tackling the fire out of her. Little did I realize that this was a very bad idea.

Apparently this girl wasn't as tough as she appeared to be. I had tackled her to the ground just about as hard as I possibly could have. She went down like a sack of potatoes. I could tell by her body language and the expression on her face that she did not take this very well at all. This proved to be fairly bad for me.

She rose up crying. I was sort of laughing at her because even though I had hit her hard; I did not think I hit her hard enough to start her bawling right in front of me. My laughter made her even more upset than before. As I turned away from her momentarily to glance at my friends (who were also giggling to themselves), she proceeded to launch herself upon my back and began to start striking me in the back of the head with her fists. Eventually after many licks to the head, a teacher came over and got her off of me.

In the end, I did not suffer any major injuries. I mainly just had a very large headache. Yeah sure, I had a little pain, but that was nothing compared to what she was apparently going through. The fight had been a full half hour ago and she was still crying. Despite all of the hitting and crying that went on, I learned an important lesson that day. No matter how tough a female may seem, you still need to treat her delicately. I have kept this firmly in mind ever since.

I Did That
E.J. Majors
Smyrna High School, Grade 10

"I did that!" That is what I say to myself when I think about my eighth grade championship football game where I helped my team win one of the biggest games of our lives. I made a very big play to help capture the title.

Smyrna Middle, the team I was on, faced Blackman for the championship. Our record was 8-0 and theirs was 7-1. Their only loss was to us in the regular season. They were determined not to let that happen again. We were tied 14-14, and Blackman had the ball on our 20 ready to score. It was close to the end of the game.

Coach Patterson pulled me to the side after a timeout and said, "Majors, you've got to make a play."

"I got you, Coach," I respond back. I was thinking to myself, *Man I have to make a play for the team, the coach, for Smyrna.* It's third down and Blackman's quarterback drops back for a pass. I see the ball in the air coming right at me and I'm thinking interception!

Right as I catch it, I repeat to myself, *Make a play…Make a play.* I break one, then another, then another tackle and head to the end zone.

"Touchdown, Smyrna!" the announcer screams.

I realize I had just run 81 yards for an interception and touchdown! Our offense goes for two, and the crowd goes crazy! The coach was so proud of me because he knew I could make the play. He had faith in our team and me. Coach Patterson is an excellent coach, and I will never forget his influence in my life.

To this day I still say, "I did that!"

Fishing Poles
Josh Carpenter
Smyrna High School, Grade 11

The glassy lake upheaves at its edges
Scents of soil and sunshine fill the morning air.
Dragonflies rehearse in a symphony of ruby, sapphire, and emerald hues as they flit about the lake's placid center.
We are silent at the end of the dock as we set our gaze on the rising sun.
The small boat rocks slightly before us and waves race across the still waters.
We settle in away from the shore.
The nature around us is rising…is waking.
I think to myself as I see the sun turn the waters to liquid gold beneath our boat.
It reminds me of El Dorado, the City of Gold.
The sparkle of metallic dew upon the leaves of the trees catches my gazing eye as I cast my line.
The bobber dances alone on the water's edge.
The morning goes on.
And the morning goes on.

Sport
Anna Elizabeth Vogler
Smyrna Elementary School, Grade 4

One fall night, my loving mom called a nice lady who was selling golden retriever puppies. She had two girls and one boy puppy. I wanted the boy because I wanted to name him Sport. So we went out to get supplies. In the morning we got ready and went to the lady's house. When we got there my puppy jumped in the car right away. That's when I met Sport. Not long down the road, Sport fell asleep in my lap. When we got home, Sport ran straight inside. That night I couldn't go to sleep. I wanted my puppy so badly.

Cheerleading
Kyndall Brooks
Thurman Francis Arts Academy, Grade 6

As soon as I tried,
I knew it was for me.
Adrenaline pumping though my veins,
Being on the verge of winning,
Standing on the mat,
Doing my best,
Knowing I can't fail.
Walking backstage,
The crowd is cheering.
It's over, I did it!
The awards ceremony is getting closer.
Now it's time, here we go.
We got first!
Now cheerleading is everything!

My Dog Black
Kristin Demonbreun
Smyrna Elementary School, Grade 5

I remember on my fifth birthday, my mom took me to Wal-mart. We were about to walk in, when we saw a box full of black puppies. I begged my mom to get one, and it was a good time to ask because we just moved into a house. She agreed and picked the smallest one. We named him Black because he was the darkest puppy. We took him home to show my big brother, who was twelve when we first got Black. He was really excited to see him. We all played with him and made him feel at home. Five months later, my mother was thinking about buying more pets so Black would have someone to play with. We bought two more dogs and two cats. Our new dogs were named Midnight, because he was darker than Black, and we named our other new dog Cocoa, because he was light brown. Our new cats were named Star and Smokey. We had them for a very long time. But when we moved back into an apartment, we took them to the woods. To this day I still wonder where they are. We didn't let Black go because he was everyone's favorite.

Christmas
Kylea Carver
Thurman Francis Arts Academy, Grade 6

Gathered around the Christmas tree
Playing "Dirty Santa."
Opening gifts, giving presents, watching people's smiles.
Laughing and smiling, joking around, having such a ball,
So much excitement, so many smiles, I just love it all.
Returning home, waiting for Santa, wondering when he will arrive
What will I get, what will it be, it will be such a surprise.
So much fun on Christmas night, so many thoughts on my mind
So many great memories I will never forget,
That will never escape my mind.

My Level 6 Year
Hannah Tomlinson
Thurman Francis Arts Academy, Grade 6

My level 6 year
We went there and here
With my friends we had so much fun
But the best thing of all is that a state meet I won.

From flips on the beam
To flips in the air
We now have memories to share.

Around the bar
Over the vault
Land on your feet or do a somersault
First on beam and all-around
Now level 7 is where I will be found.

Memories: Beautiful Scenes
Robyn Sharp
Thurman Francis Arts Academy, Grade 7

Sunning on the beach:
Beautiful scenery ahead of me
The vastness of the ocean
Hits me like a magic potion
I'll never leave; I'll always stay
Oh please, Mom, don't take me away.

Camping at the lake:
Beautiful scenery ahead of me
Trees covering the land in miles
The boat brings my family smiles
I love camping, the vibe I feel
It's much better than even a home-cooked meal.

Sightseeing at Fall Creek Falls:
Beautiful scenery ahead of me
The jagged mountains above my head
Powerful waterfalls allow the soil to be fed
My family and I, having a blast
Look at that eagle, it's flying so fast.

Vacationing in South Africa:
Beautiful scenery ahead of me
The peaceful fields, filled with goats
All the working children who have no coats
Mountains, valleys, rivers, animals, and people
Sitting and playing under the church steeple.

Skiing in Copper Mountain, Colorado:
Beautiful scenery ahead of me
As I swish down the mountain on my skies
I look so cool, till I fall on my knees
After our laughs, we head down
Being with my family, I can't get out of town.

Beautiful scenery ahead of me
It's everywhere, just look around and you will see
Beautiful scenery is in you and me
In your visions you can trust
The memories of love inside of us.

Chapter Four

Life's Handprints

Hope
Brent Nevar
Central Middle School, Grade 8

Hope is when you have nothing and yet persevere,
Working for a better tomorrow
Hope is being positive
When everything around you is overflowing with negativity.
Hope is the end of the old
And a chance for a new beginning
Hope is seeing the light
Even through the darkest cave
Hope is totally inspiring.

Not Just a Handprint
Siori Koerner
Christiana Middle School, Grade 8

At first glance nobody would suspect
That we have ever talked or even laughed
But you have not only left a handprint
You have taken and run with it to the ends of time
My heart

When we first met, we were both awkward
You with your poofy hair and me with my scowl
But we have not only managed to get along
We have had only the best times together
My friend

I will never forget the lessons you have taught me
Whether they were intentional or not
Neither of us will ever forget
The laughs, the fights, and
The tears

Now as freshman year approaches
And new beginnings await us
I hope our adventures never end
And our friendship will continue to blossom
My soul-sister

At first glance nobody would suspect
That we have ever talked or even laughed
But you have not only left a handprint
You have taken and run with it to the ends of time
My heart

Handprint on My Heart
Rebecca Lopez
Christiana Middle School, Grade 8

Every moving second,
In this limited thing called life,
Somebody has left a handprint on my heart,
My best friend,
The spontaneous, Siori.

She has always been there for me,
When I did not feel quite right.
Siori has always known,
How to make me feel better.

We have been through highs and lows,
But we will always be BFF's.
We have had great times together,
Laughing and enjoying life.

Whenever I have had issues,
Siori has always been there,
To give me a tissue.
This is why she has left a handprint on my heart,
She has always been there for me.

Jenny Peters • Thurman Francis Arts Academy • Grade 2

Safe Haven Family Shelter
Meredith Mills
Rock Springs Middle School, Grade 6

One thing that really touched my heart is when I went to Safe Haven Family Shelter to serve food. Safe Haven Family Shelter is a homeless shelter for families with children who have had some bad luck. Maybe the parents have lost a job or gone through a divorce. All of the children still have to go to school like normal kids. Everyone seemed to be very content and at home at the shelter. Here are some of the reasons why I was touched by the experience.

First, there are lots of kids there in need. All of the kids hugged us and welcomed us right in. Whenever I think back on this experience, I always say to myself *That could have been me*. Those children are very thankful for every little thing they have, and I need to start being more like them.

Second, I think it is wonderful that the shelter lets families stay together. I always wonder how children who live in foster homes move on without family. If I were homeless, it would make me feel better to be with my family. It's awesome, because, unlike most shelters, this shelter helps the parents find jobs after they leave. They also help families manage money and find homes. This shelter is a wonderful place!

Finally, Safe Haven Family Shelter is like a real home. For example, there are house rules; lights go off at ten o'clock. Everyone has chores and duties, both kids and adults. There are also rooms in the shelter like a real house. It is a very homey place!

As you can see, this experience has really changed the way I think, treat others, and react to situations. I am a lot more thankful for my friends, family, food, water, and shelter. I will continue to help the shelter and give food. I am praying that all of the families, not just at the shelter but all homeless families, find nice homes, jobs, and futures.

The Heart's Canvas
Caitlin Lee
Oakland High School, Grade 12

Every passing moment
Leaves a mark you cannot see.
A small mark on your heart
Like a teardrop swallowed by the sea.
You may not notice it.
You may even forget it,
But the mark is there all the same
Every meeting, every word, and every minute
Leaves a mark like a splash of paint.
A person's heart is a blank canvas
Just waiting to be painted
By life's colorful vibrance.

I Do Not Understand
Daniel Graham
Daniel McKee Alternative School, Grade 11

I do not understand
    Why the grass is green
    Why the water is blue
    Why humans walk on their feet and not their hands
But most of all
    I do not understand why people bully other people
    (I've seen a person be thrown into a locker
     because his glasses were too big)
What I understand most are robots
    They don't argue
    They don't talk (unless you program them to)
    All they do is obey their master.

Chasing
Shelby Bolton
Smyrna High School, Grade 12

We burn, we bleed, we cry, we grieve,
we smile, we play, we chase the day.
We dig the graves of those who
haven't touched our lives.
Our "work" is called hiding,
although the pain is inescapable.
We cuss, we think, we're driven to the brink,
we hunt, we thrive, somehow we manage
to stay alive.
Our tears are dried by the wind,
and our scars map out just how agonizing
our journey has been,
yet we continue to carry the forgotten memories.
We yell, we scream, we deliver the dream,
we turn, we pray, and continue chasing the day.

Understand?
Chianti Hill
Daniel McKee Alternative School, Grade 9

I do not understand
Why people believe they have a right to abuse others
Why they forsake the ones they love for the ones they like
Why popularity defines you in the world
But most of all
I do not understand
Why when a voice cries out in the night
No one cares if it's heard
Why others try to hold you back from the
One who cares and loves you
Why when you're young you get pushed to the side
And told you're always wrong
What I do understand is
How to love those who get turned away
For the wrong reasons
How to hold my head up high
When things go wrong
That everyone young and old
Has a voice that should be heard
What it feels like to be torn in two
To feel like no one's there
What it feels like to love and be loved.
I understand. Do you?

Handprint on My Heart
Virginia Tipps
Christiana Middle School, Grade 7

Hallee, among many other people, has left a handprint on my heart.
On my heart is an imprint of this great friend.
When two young girls met in pre-school they shared a world of fun,
Birthdays, parties, play dates, and sleepovers,
Our first concert, or ride in a limo.
Our first sleepover and our first Halloween together.
Our first good-bye, and in a way our last moment with each other.
Hallee, you taught me that we do not know how much you love someone until they are gone.
Hallee, you may not still be here on earth with me, but you will always be with me
As a handprint on my heart.

Handprint on My Heart
Mason Shadrick
Christiana Middle School, Grade 7

He is all there was
He is all there is
He is all there will be
He is Jesus, the handprint on my heart.

He made me a happier person
He made me a nicer person
He made me a better person
He is Jesus, the handprint on my heart.

He has helped me get smarter
He has helped me get stronger
He has helped me grow
He is Jesus, the handprint on my heart.

He is the One who is God
He is the One who has forgiven me for my sins
He is the One I love
He is Jesus, the handprint on my heart.

Loving Life
Bryan Beyal
Central Middle School, Grade 8

Life without love would be dull
Love without life is dead
We live to love
We love to live
Without life there would be no love
Without love there would be no life

Hope
Esther Soper
Central Middle School, Grade 7

Hope is to love
or want something so much that you never let go.
Hope is the belief
that things can only get better.
Hope is the thing
that can keep you going in even the darkest seemingly most hopeless of times.
Hope is that hidden strength
we find deep within ourselves for our family.
And when things look bleak,
when our heart is broken,
when you feel you can't go on,
Hope is the flashlight, the duct tape, and the best friend
pushing you in your little red wagon.
Hope is your energizer bunny
And hope is in all of us…

Three-Part Heart
Kandace Clark
Central Middle School, Grade 8

It started off as footprints
The friendship was slow
Taking one step at a time
So the relationship could grow
I never knew…two people
Could mean more to me
Than my close-knit family
Not only sharing hard times
But eternal memories
The footprints were getting closer
Till we were all on the same path
Our bond was close
Our feet not only matched
But our minds were in the same place,
On the same path
Sisters we are now,
You'll never see us apart
For those footprints
Soon became
Handprints on my heart.
Best friends… forever.

Handprints on My Heart
Collinthia House
Central Middle School, Grade 8

I remember running. Yes, I run to win but more for other reasons. I run to be free. Free from all the struggle and worry. When I run, I don't have to think about what people think of me. I don't have to act differently. I don't have to pretend. It's just me, the ground, and everyone around me just fades away. The loud roar of the crowd slips away like a coma. At the start command, I tingle with anticipation. "Runners, set." Like a car engine I rev up. "Pop," goes the gun. I sprint and it's like I have left my fake shell there alone. I look back. It waves, but it knows it will be back. I pass everyone with ease. Step. Step. Step. I get into a beat. Then I see the finish line, and it all rushes in. The yells sound like a blob. I finish and slip back into my uneasy shell.

Rocky, the Great Horse!
Abby Cerna
Cedar Grove Elementary School, Grade 1

I love horses! I ride Rocky every Saturday. Rocky is the best horse I have ever seen. He is fast and tall. He obeys my commands. He eats a lot of hay, carrots, and apples. I love him because he makes my day the best day ever!

The First Day of Second Grade
Lauren Miller
Buchanan Elementary School, Grade 5

It was the first day of second grade and I was waiting for the yellow bus to come and pick me up. I was a little scared but, my mom said, "You have to go to school!" When the huge, yellow bus finally arrived, I entered it. As I got on the gigantic bus, I saw a pretty girl sitting alone. She had gorgeous, curly, brown hair with beautiful, blue eyes. There was nowhere else to sit, so I asked to sit with her. She said, "Of course you can sit here." So I took my pink, polka-dotted bag off my back and sat down on the seat. I asked her what her name was and she said, "Megan, and your name is?"

I replied to her by saying, "I am Lauren, and I am in the second grade."

"Me too!" Megan shouted. We started talking, and I was so glad to sit with her. "Do you want to be my friend?" I said with a great big smile on my face.

"I would love to be your friend!" Megan yelled as I handed her a shiny, bright pink friendship bracelet. The bracelet I gave Megan was the same pink bracelet I had around my wrist. The only thing we were upset about was that we weren't in the same class. At least we rode the same bus, and we would see each other every day. That day Megan was very hyper. She was so funny! Megan would say random words like "caterpillar." I told her that she was crazy, and she said, "Thank you!"

She started bouncing on the bus seat so I said, "Maybe we should get something to hold you down." We both laughed loudly. Then the bus stopped and we went inside to the cafeteria. Since we were in different classes, we sat at different tables in the cafeteria. Megan said "I will see you later at recess!"

I said, "Okay, can't wait!" We both sat down waiting for the time to pass. Then our wonderful teachers came to get us. I waved to Megan and she waved back. Then I walked to the colorful classroom with my class. Her class was walking beside mine. I watched her enter her classroom as I entered mine. The day passed by and then it was finally time for recess. Megan's class was already on the playground, and she was waiting for me.

When I got on the huge, bright yellow bus with my pink polka-dotted backpack that first day of second grade, I didn't know what was going to happen next. That day changed my life in a way I didn't expect. I made a new friend that I would keep for many years. I am now in fifth grade and we are still friends. We have been through a lot together and I know we will always be friends no matter what.

The Horrible Social Studies Paper!
Katie Lang
Buchanan Elementary School, Grade 5

There I was, sitting in my school chair, looking at the number 68 on my social studies paper. I couldn't help but wonder what to tell my parents when I got home and showed them this awful paper. Then, I thought to myself, I probably don't have to show them. I started realizing that I could think of some ways to help me make a good decision. I mean, it's probably the right thing to show them, but I still didn't want to. "Darn," I whispered to myself. Then, I took my water bottle and swallowed a big gulp.

When our class was finished with science, we started a new lesson in social studies. I tried to pay close attention to what the teacher was saying, but then the teachers quizzed us orally. The quiz was on certain things we needed to remember on this chapter. I kept on raising my hand every time the teacher asked the class a question, because the answer went right into my head. At the end of the day, my friend, Kassidy, asked me, "So what did you get on you social studies test today?"

"Oh, that's right!" I groaned. Then I started having the feeling that I was going to burst out crying. I screamed inside my head, *I don't know what I'm going to do yet!* Suddenly, the principal called on the speaker and said that he hoped everyone had a good day and that he would be back shortly for dismissal. After that, I got super nervous about what I was going to do. So, I stopped and thought about it. *Hummm.* Now what would happen if I didn't show my parents the test and threw it away instead? I had this terrible thought; if I didn't show them, I would keep doing badly in social studies and fail. Also, they would find out eventually, and I would be in even more trouble. However, if I did show them, I could boost my grade to an awesome "A" and that's what I want. I thought that the second idea would be the better choice. Then, the principal called on the speaker and dismissed car riders. *Here we go*, I worried.

I took a deep breath when I saw my mom in her car. I slowly walked to the car, and we went home. When we arrived, I sadly shuffled toward my mommy and daddy. When I gave them the horrible paper, I started crying. Unexpectedly, they gave me a hug and said, "Honey, if you needed help in social studies, you should have told us. Please don't cry." All of a sudden, I thought about the decision I had made. My tears dried up, and I immediately felt proud of myself for making the right choice. What I had done will be a good start for my future, because it will help me make bigger decisions than this one.

Best Friends
Taryn Taylor
Buchanan Elementary School, Grade 8

All the drama there used to be
All the late night phone calls
All the laughs and funny insiders we used to have
Every picture we took we said was ugly and how much we hated it
As long as we were together, nothing else mattered
We both love how everyone would say,
 "They'll be best friends until the end of time," or
 "They're always together."
And here we still are: best friends.

What Love Is
Jessica Farler
Buchanan Elementary School, Grade 6

Love is pure
Love is kind
Love can always change your mind
Love is nice
Love is sweet
Love can help you meet
Love is strange
Love is cool
Love will sometimes make you a fool
But the most important thing of all is that
Love will always be in your
Heart

To Have
Brittney West
Buchanan Elementary School, Grade 6

To have is to dream
to dream is to love
To love is to cherish
to cherish is to be peaceful
To have peace is to care
to care is to imagine
To have imagination is to inspire
to inspire is to take chances
To have chances is to wish
to wish is to be kind
To have kindness is to be thoughtful
to be thoughtful is to create
To have creativity is to have responsibility
to have responsibility is to have rights
To have rights is to be equal
to be equal is to be fair
To have fairness is to share
to share is to give
These are the things we need...
To have.

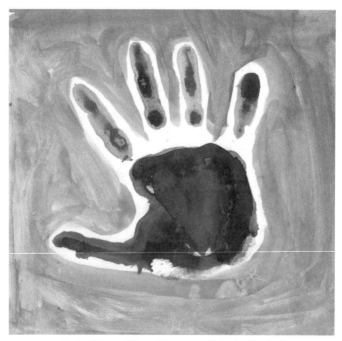

Katie Goins • Wilson Elementary School • Grade 4

The Turning of Hearts
Austin Poteete
Blackman High School, Grade 11

All the seasons I have seen through teary eyes,
To have loved and lost they say, but still I dismay,
For my many failed attempts, I cannot take the suspense,
Will this time I succeed or once again will I bleed,
To have tried only to fail, to have given all to no avail,
This never ending circle of pain, it has left on me a vicious stain,
With all this happiness to gain, it seems all I'll ever know is pain,
Broken and tired I give up, I give in, upon the end it shall begin,
For lying shattered on the floor, he steps through the open door,
Bright and brilliant is his visage, I could not have dreamt a more perfect image,
This radiance I have not felt,
Still my worries lie unseen,
But for now I will forsake my urge to flee, to hope that this time I will succeed,
A love requited is a blissful thing, not to fear your venomous sting,
For all the stains you left on me, he is willing to make clean,
All the scars they fade away, finally all your transgressions I forgave,
I don't resent anymore, for when he stepped in he closed that door,
I will not miss you ever again,
I have learned to trust, forgive, and love.
Because of this I am restored.

Worrying
Emyle Lawrence
Blackman High School, Grade 11

Lying awake not able to sleep
Tossing and turning
Unable to weep
Wondering where you are
And why you haven't called
Regretting the words that we shared
Ashamed and feeling scared
Why do you do this to me?
You know how much I care
Why do you leave me feeling alone and scared
Lying awake unable to sleep
Tired of worrying and weeping
I don't care anymore
Live your life the way you want
I'm done

Shaken Waters, Still Land
Sara Wylie Helton
Blackman Middle School, Grade 7

>Handprints on my heart
>Are like footprints in the sand
>
>Wading in the water
>Walking on the land
>
>When I'm not with you I wander
>With an open brain I ponder
>
>Just seeing you smile
>Helps me go the extra mile
>
>The feeling that abides
>While you walk by my side
>
>The tears that push through
>When I can't be noticed by you
>
>The love I share for you will forever stand
>Because I know I am in good hands

Not All Things
Andario Howard
Oakland High School, Grade 12

>Not all things last forever.
>The bright sun eventually is overwhelmed by the darkness of the night.
>The monstrous waves of the broad seas are calmed by the boundaries of the land.
>The vibrant leaves that hang lively on the trees eventually fall lifelessly to the ground
>Childhood pastimes age to become nothing but memories.
>Even life itself comes to an abrupt halt at some point.
>Not all things are intended to last forever; however, the impression that you left
>On my heart is everlasting.

Those People in Life
Madison Baird
Blackman Middle School, Grade 8

Do you have those people in life
Who are always there for you?
No matter the distance in miles,
No matter the distance in inches.

Do you have those people in life
Where time flies too fast when you're together?
Where it seems like just yesterday you were together,
And yet a week has already passed?

Do you have those people in life
Who wipe away your tears?
Who are there for your happiness and laughter,
Your anger and sadness.

Do you have those people in life
Who are there despite your health?
Despite your flaws,
Who look past your differences.

Do you have those people in life
Who make you feel completely happy?
The ones who make you feel you can make a change in the world,
Those you make you want to make a change in the world?

Do you have those people in life
Who bring you up when you are down?
The ones you care so deeply about,
The ones you worry about every hour of every day.

Do you have those people in life
Who make you ask yourself, "Is this right or wrong?"
The ones you'd do anything for,
And expect nothing in return?

I have those people in my life.
They know who they are;
They know that I'll love them
Forever and for always.

Friends
Denis Korobkov
Oakland High School, Grade 12

A group of people to call your best friends
Ones you know will stay 'til the end.
These wonderful years have been so surreal
From all this I have learned so much.
To these friends of mine I award all of my trust.
And now our time together is shrinking;
Yet I cannot commit to stop thinking
Thank you, my friends, for this magnificent art
That of which is a handprint upon my heart.

Are You Still Here?
Alexandria Hunter
McFadden School of Excellence, Grade 8

If I can't hear your voice, are you still here with me?
If I only listen for the thunder, can the whisper still set me free?
If my idea of perfection is not what you want for me,
Will you give me my selfish wish, or open my eyes that I may see?

If I can't feel you with me, are you still by my side?
Do you know who I really am, even though I hide?
If all I want is beauty, but you have different eyes
Will I get what I want, and hide myself in another disguise?

If I don't think you're listening, do you still hear what I say?
Can I trust you to care for me each and every day?
If I trust you wholly, and from your paths never stray,
Will you keep me with you, so I don't fall away?

If I can't feel your love, will you show me it's there?
When everything is going wrong, will you keep me from despair?
If I give you my life, you will lead me where
All my fears have gone away, and nothing can compare.

Will You Be There?
Courtney Goodman
McFadden School of Excellence, Grade 8

When I am torn
And have been thrown
Will you be there
To take me home?

When I am lost
And get off track
Will you be there
To bring me back?

When I am alone
With my heart beyond mend
Will you be there
To be my friend?

When I am scared
So frightened I can't stand
Will you be there
To hold my hand?

Because I will soon
Fall victim to this woe
I need you to love me
And never let go

When I am going
Getting ready to ascend
Will you be there
'Till the very end?

He Is
Griffin Dodd
McFadden School of Excellence, Grade 6

He is almighty yet merciful
He is unborn yet all-knowing
He wields power no man can imagine yet he loves us as if we were his
New born children
He watches over us in all ways
If I were a warhorse,
He would guide me through battle
If I were a kite,
He would make sure I landed safely
If I were a boy in a world of greed and hate,
He would see I lived my life in peace
He even sent his Son to die on the cross not for humanity, but for you and me

        He is…God

The Pet I Love
Sydney Barnett
McFadden School of Excellence, Kindergarten

I love my guinea pig. Her name is Lille. She likes to bite my dad's fegr.

Mollie Stone • Blackman Elementary School • Grade 2

My Dream
Emma Arnette
McFadden School of Excellence, Grade 6

Desks…books…pencils…erasers… are what I envision in my dream of becoming an elementary school teacher. I want to keep the tradition alive of becoming a teacher. My grandmother was and my mom is a teacher. I want to become a teacher because I like helping and teaching other people how to become better at something. In my opinion, teaching is a rewarding career.

My earliest memory is of me playing school. I dressed in high heels, bracelets, huge earrings, and skirts. I have collected lots of teaching materials over the years that I use frequently. These include old teacher's manuals, animal posters, and workbooks. I have even been known to wear fake glasses! My mom always says that she never has to worry about my teacher's teaching style, because I tend to become that person. For example, my third grade teacher always wore lots of bracelets; so, I wore bracelets when I played school, too. My fifth grade teacher wore jackets often. So can you guess what I did? By the way, I blame teachers for getting me started on coffee drinking.

During the summer months, you might just find me in my mom's classroom writing on the overhead or doing graphic organizers on the easel. Or I might be in the rocking chair doing a read aloud. I might have failed to mention that I still have every book I have ever gotten (board books included). Being in a classroom is one of my favorite pastimes.

I have all the materials I need to get started, but some of the qualities I will need to learn. Patience, for example, is something that will help me become a better teacher. Good teachers need to be creative which is another area in which I strive to improve. Knowledge is another area in which I have to improve. When I am a teacher I will try my best to be a helpful, patient, and trustworthy teacher.

As you can tell teaching is my lifelong dream. I plan to teach fifth grade and continue the tradition.

What Have I Become?
Eli Ragland
McFadden School of Excellence, Grade 6

While my life may seem great when you are looking at me
It really is not all that easy
I don't really know what I'm feeling inside
Because life has taken me for a bumpy ride
I have too many handprints on my heart
It's being overused; everyone's taking a part
Don't know what to do, don't know what to say
Don't know what I'd do if I did anyway
Sometimes I'm mad or solely depressed
Sometimes I just want to stay home and rest
Who am I, can I figure myself out?
What have I become; what am I about?
Who am I to be wasting my time,
While others are pitiful and don't make a dime
I'm at my limit; I've hit a wall
Sometimes it seems like I can't do it all
I'm rushing through life, but I want it to stop
I'm climbing through emotions and can't get to the top
I am locked inside me
But I don't want to be
My world's gone obscure
But I don't have the cure

Touched My Heart
Mason Nolan
McFadden School of Excellence, Grade 1

My dog really touches my heart. I like it when my dog lays her head on me. She licks me when I come home from school She runs to see me.

Dig Inside Your Heart
Nathan Clark
McFadden School of Excellence, Grade 3

Dig inside your heart,
You don't need a chart.
From back in Georgia,
To here in Tennessee.
From being a rock star,
To just driving a car.
You will find your family,
I'm glad they raised me tamely.

This Way
La'Shay Johnson-Clay
LaVergne Middle School, Grade 8

Nowadays, folks never say I love you,
They act like they don't know how to.
No good mornings, good nights or I'll miss you,
And your kids are afraid to kiss you.

Our hearts aren't the sizes they used to be,
Takes too long opening up,
And you'll lose the key,
Your hard drive will eventually lose all your precious memories,
Your friends might even sell you for parts,
At least then you'll know who on your list is off the charts.
But love the folks who love you,
Then, at least, you'll still have an ounce of hope and love in your heart.

Enough to get you up the mountain and back,
Just don't forget whom not to pack.

Promise yourself you'll never give up,
On those who are there for you.
This way someone might hear you and learn not to be so cruel,
This way your best friend and you won't remember that harsh duel,
And this way, when you go to sleep, you will feel good about you.
And that way, you can finally say
I love you.

Friends Argue
Taylor Canter
LaVergne Primary School, Kindergarten

Trisha and I got in an argument.
It was her turn to pick the game.
She picked the game and I feel better.
Because she picked hide-n-seek.

U.S.A. Heart to Heart and Hand to Hand
Gabriel Pledger
LaVergne Middle School, Grade 8

Heart to heart hand to hand
United as one we stand.
This country was forged of blood, sweat, and tears.
Across the world people lend us their ears.
To hear a story of a nation that beat the odds
For we were the underdogs.
Now on top of the world we stand heart to heart
And hand to hand.

Karys Goostree • Brown's Chapel Preschool

America Is a Place
Rachel Yates
LaVergne High School, Grade 10

America is where it's free
Where we sleep in peace
It's where our children play
And it's a place where...
We
Pray
We
Grow
We
Live

Handprints on Heart Story
Addison Gentry
LaVergne Middle School, Grade 6

  Have you ever met someone who ends up being one of your best friends and it all happens surprisingly? Have you ever been able to relate to that one person so well? Well, I have and that person's name is Aaliyah.
  My sister Skylar and I were only starting second and fourth grade, and we were driving to our mema's house for dinner. We had stopped the car, and of course, Skylar and I had run like crazy over the front yard until our Mom started unlocking the door. Then Skylar and I stood on the porch beside our Mom.
  Suddenly, a big, silver van stopped in front of the house. We all stared as a young woman with long, blonde hair got out and started walking towards us.
  When she was right in front of us, she smiled and said, "Hello, I'm Diana. I live just down the street. My daughter, Aaliyah, keeps noticing your girls playing in the backyard and would like to play with them sometime." She smiled, and Skylar and I instantly nodded.
  Mom looked at Skylar and I then at Diana. "Sure!" Mom said. "We'll try to get together soon."
  Diana smiled again and quickly wrote her address down on a piece of paper. "Here," she said and gave Mom the paper. "Thank you so much! Bye!" She drove away.
  Skyler and I grinned and ran inside to go and tell our mema. We were so happy!
  A week later, Skylar and I were spending the night at our mema's house. We were watching television when we heard a knock at the door.
  "I wonder who that is?" Mema said hurrying toward the door.
  As soon as she opened it, there stood Diana, her husband Mike, her son Maliches, and Aaliya. "Hi!" said Aaliyah.

Painful Memories
Elizabeth Davenport
Lascassas Elementary School, Grade 7

A young boy
In a family of five
A new little sprout.

A growing toddler
She's a budding blossom
In a family of four.

A thunderstorm
On a day in May
Ramping and raging.

Two cars on the road
One family in each car
Lightening strikes a tree.

The two cars swerve and collide.
The sound of the collision
Lost in the rumbling of thunder.

Each family suffered a loss.
Each family mourned.
Each family helped the other.

The baby boy and the little girl
All grown up
Share the losses with each other.

A thunderstorm
On a day in May
Reminds me of what happened.

Autumn Falls
Amisha Mitchell
Lascassas Elementary School, Grade 5

Autumn is finally here
All the trees are bare
It's time to wear blue jeans and jackets
Time to rake leaves as the squirrels pick up acorns
And scramble up the trees.
Fall is here!
Fall is here!
Let everyone cheer because
Fall is here!

Night
Tanner Jones
Lascassas Elementary School, Grade 5

I wish this night,
Would hurry and turn to light,
For it is giving me a fright.

I can't even get up
To get a quick bite.

I'm too scared,
I wish I would,
Be more prepared.

I wish this night,
Would turn to light,
For it is giving me a fright.

Then I go to sleep,
With a creep,
I make it through the night until
I awake, and then
It is light.

Ode to Our Teacher

Savannah Berry and Lindsay Randolph
Lascassas Elementary School, Grade 5

Each day of our lives,
There are chances to take,
Things to learn and decisions to make.

We adore our teacher
Ever so much
We love the magic of
Her tender touch.

When we feel the world spinning,
Needing to slow down
Our teacher's gentle voice is there
To bring us back around.

Handprints

Nicholas Emerton
Kittrell Elementary School, Grade 8

Her only light in the bright of our future far
Away from yet knowing all of life and
Nature's secrets to success
Daring and
Primitive he may seem but don't be deceived by
Regal
Images for
Nothing can be as
Truly appetizing as the
Suspense of what he may do

The Pony
Mollie McDonald
Lascassas Elementary School, Grade 5

When I was seven years old, I begged my parents for a pony every day. I also prayed for one every night. One morning I went to the side door and I saw one of our horses out. I told Mom and Dad, and Dad hopped on the four-wheeler and rode down to the barn.

When he rode back, he said it wasn't one of our horses so he put it alone in our little pen. He said the pony was really gentle. He also said he was outside of our gate.

I asked if we could keep him. But Dad said we had to find its owners. I was pretty bummed, so we sat there. Then, a van came zooming down our driveway. He parked and we ran toward him.

"Hi," we greeted him.

"Hi," the old man said. "Anybody seen my stallion?" It was kind of funny because he said stallion.

"Yes," Dad answered. "He's down there."

"Oh," he said. "Would you folks want him? My girls don't ride him anymore."

My face lit up. "Please, please, please?" I asked, looking up expectantly at mom and dad.

"Wellllll," dad said. "We don't have the papers or his things."

"Yes, I do," the old man said, opening his van door. He had all his things in there.

I looked up again. "Please, please, please?" I asked again.

"Well, okay," they said. "What's his name?"

"Chili bean," he answered.

"Yay!!!" I yelled. We filled out the papers and took his tack and the man left. We all walked down to see my new horse. We all thought about it and decided that the man planned it all. The next day, I found out that I was in the same class as one of his daughters. Her name was Katelynn. At first, she didn't believe me, but I finally convinced her.

Then every day from then on, she would ask me "Are you taking care of my horse?"

And every day I would answer, "Yes, I am!"

Impressions on My Life
Kaneisha Jordan
Kittrell School Elementary, Grade 8

Impressions like voices
Loud ones like nails on a chalkboard.
Soft ones like a whisper
through the air on a windy day.
Deep like a base on a brand new drum set.
High ones like birds chirping
at dawn.
Impressions like voices.

Impressions as in colors
Black as in the scary dark nightmares.
Red as in the blood shed from all the
stumbles we make in life.
Blue as in the blue pen used
To correct all your life mistakes.
Gold as in gold stars you deserve for
all your accomplishments
you've done.
Orange as in fruits and veggies you shove on the floor when they turn their heads.
Impressions as in colors

Impressions like shapes
Circles like the round trip
We make to find our self.

Squares as in the TV's
We sit and watch while
Life passes by.
Triangles like the
Tent we build when
We're 4 and 5
Stars as in the stars
In the sky that we
Stair at and think
Life through.
Rectangles like the mirrors
We gaze into because we have
To look right to the world
Impressions.

Impressions as in words
Friend as in people who
Smile in your face then

Talk behind your back.
Best as in right and never
Wrong even if you try your hardest.
Truth as in what you
Want to hear
Wrong as in not what you
Got.
Love as in my heart has fallen
Head over hills, through a lake pass
The valley and back again.
Impressions as in words.

Impressions on my life!

Lindsay Wick • Oakland High School • Grade 12

Sweet Dreams
Katelyn Worley
Kittrell Elementary School, Grade 2

I'm only eight and you'd never guess
The sport I like to do the best.
My brother started and I followed soon
I have a tractor with stars and a moon.
Number 112 is yellow and blue
My daddy built it from scratch brand new.
I wanted to call it Drama Queen from the start
Instead it's Sweet Dreams and she has my heart.
The goal is to pull weight in dirt and sand
I have to pull it as far as I can.
I have support from my family and friends
Mom and Dad like it when I win.
Aunts, uncles, cousins, and grandparent,s too
Like to come watch me win or lose.
It's not the money or trophies, it's the release of the clutch
It's the pull of the engine that I love so much.
Three years of fun, ten months a year
I compete in Tennessee far and near.
I can't wait to start back for the Worley Pulling Team,
But until then I'll have Sweet Dreams.

Why?
Ciera Powers
Holloway High School, Grade 12

Why May 28? Why 2007? Why did I have to be there? Why didn't I cover you and take that bullet? Why did you have to die while I escaped without a scratch? I watched you take your last breath. Your blood drenching my socks! Your face was so peaceful; the only sign of tragedy was the blood rolling from your ear. I remember that day so vividly…I made you a T-bone steak with peppers and onions. If only I had known that it would be your last meal…Your smile remains in my memory. Your Chinese eyes that often glared at me! The way you just chilled ALL DAY and seemed like you didn't have a care in the world! We had it rough growing up, yet you never let it show…I know you were hurting inside just like me…But emotions equal weakness, that was our philosophy. Man, it seems like just yesterday we were wrestling and boxing in the kitchen and bribing each other with cigarettes to wash the dishes. We were poor as hell, but we kept cigarettes…You hated the way I ran the streets, and I ignored you and neglected you. I put money before you and your feelings. I wish I had it all to do over…I would hug and kiss you every minute and let you know how much I loved you. I've got nothing but memories now…I wish you could see me now and the person that I've become! I'm determined to make you proud. Even though you're dead and gone…You will always be my twin sister and best friend!

Christmas
Kalyn Patterson
Eagleville School, Grade 8

It is seven A.M. and I have just awakened.
The smell of bacon and eggs creeps
up the stairs trying to force me down.
"Kalyn!" My mom was calling me downstairs.
"Kalyn, come on; it's a surprise!"

As I looked out the window, the earth had
gone colorless overnight. I jump down the
stairs, begging my parents to tell me
what the surprise was. Then
something caught my eye.

It's beautiful. It's just what I wanted.
And it's from Santa....himself!!

I couldn't believe my eyes. The letter I sent to Santa
actually made it to the North Pole. I stood
there and tried to speak but nothing came
out of my mouth. I was in awe of
what I just found out.

Santa really does exist!!

A Boy and a Poem
Marty Council
Eagleville School, Grade 12

There once was a boy who needed a poem for class,
And the last thing he wanted was to hear his teacher's sass.
So he sat there and he thought,
And he thought till his head hurt,
Then he scribbled something down and hoped it worked.
The bell rang and he took it to class,
The room was full and to the mass.
As the teacher walked in, she told them to "hush."
Then the fire alarm went off and everybody got up in a rush.
Then the boy thought to himself as he went down the hall,
He didn't need the poem after all.

Pasture Full
Hunter Faulk
Eagleville School, Grade 12

Beautiful open field, tall dried grass
Looking as if to be grain
Wide open range of view
Nothing but horse's cantor and short breaths
This for me is a place of peace
When only the horses and I matter
Nothing but pure freedom
I cannot think of a more wonderful place to be
Beautiful palomino, beast of power and grace
This is my pasture of peace.

Flight
Doug Brown
Rock Springs Middle School, Grade 7

Soaring through the air
At unimaginable speeds
The wind going through your hair
You fly above the tops of trees

The way you take off
You feel as free as a bird
It is suddenly very quiet
Not a sound is heard

But when you are landing
And your journey is done
You lie down to rest
And prepare for another one

This is how I felt
When I flew my first time
In that small little sports craft
For thirty minutes of time

I Once Told a Friend
Morgan Rhoades
Riverdale High School, Grade 12

Mind-numbing, heart-breaking pain
Tears streaming down his face
This is not the time to have nothing to say
So I tried really hard to make the silence break
The words came out like I had said it before
And here are my words that broke this war
You lose what wants to be lost
You gain what wants to be found
And you live life the way you want to live
The tears slowly stopped
And he looked at me in awe
Like he realized that life could actually move on
His heart was still broken and his mind was still numb
But the silence was broken and his goal was to move on
I will never forget those words I said to this friend
Because his goal was accomplished and his happiness was regained

Checkers
Allie Davis
Riverdale High School, Grade 12

Life is like a game of checkers,
Once you go forward,
You can't go back,
Once you get to the other side,
You can go anywhere.

You Saved Me
Alejandra Carrillo
Smyrna High School, Grade 11

I am alone in the dark room as I scramble
To pick up the pieces of my life, frantically trying to keep
Myself together, to not lose control.
Outside a storm rages, inside the walls constrict.
The howling wind swirls into the room,
Flinging the pieces along the way,
Wreaking havoc, destroying everything in its path.
Can't take any more!
I curl up on the floor, hands pressed against my ears.
The battle is lost, I am lost, until... silence.
The storm, the howling, the swirling, stop.
The pieces fall gently to the floor.
The constricted room, no longer black, expands.
Slowly, I raise my head.
I meet your warm eyes, your bright smile.
Relief at last, the storm has passed.
You help me up.
You walk by my side, lighting up the way.
Hand-in-hand we pick up the broken pieces,
Rebuilding my life with your glue.
You saved me.

Heather Allen • Siegel High School • Grade 10

Target Practice
Kaitlyn Whittle
Smyrna High School, Grade 11

Aim for the sky
they say;
but if you do
how will you catch the arrow?

don't aim too low
they say;
understandable to me
considering you'll just hit your foot

aim just right
I say;
because it's in grasping distance
you just have to jump to catch it

Meant to Be
Tabitha Smitty
Smyrna High School, Grade 9

You make me smile
You help me breathe
I'm going my mile
Because you made me strong underneath

You held me near
When no one else would
I loved you so dear
When no one else could

Do you truly understand
What I'm saying to you
While I'm grabbing your hand
You're grabbing mine too

While my world was falling apart
You were always there
You stole my heart
And got me in such a scare

I love the feeling you gave me
When I was with you
That's why we're meant to be
And you know you're thinking it, too.

My Game
Katie Williams
Smyrna High School, Grade 12

Basketball is the name of the best game
Five on five, these days is how it is played
If you believe in yourself, shoot and aim
Play poor defense and you might just get sprayed

Good practice makes perfect, that's how it goes
All in preparation of the season
Work on 3 pointers, lay-ups, and free throws
The pain and sweat is all for a reason

Play every single game like it is your last
The score, fouls, and free throws count in the end
Dribble hard down the court swiftly and fast
Guard your opponent tightly and defend

All these things I have overcome and faced
My love for the game can't be replaced

The Perfect Words
Brittany Maxwell
Smyrna High School, Grade 11

"Why are you frightened?"
Your query whispered so low and tender.
I struggled to find the words to say,
Because I knew it would be the day,
We would always remember.
I always wanted to tell you,
But I needed the right words.
I wanted it to be perfect,
So as to ensure we would be together,
Forever.
Before I knew what I was saying,
I whispered in reply:
"I am frightened because I love you."
I then slowly turned and walked away.

Change
Reggie Pierre-Paul
Smyrna High School, Grade 11

Things don't change, we do
The world stays the same no matter the time or place
Attitudes are like paintbrushes
Painting every situation we face
Emotions come and go
Hatred, sadness, fear
Cravings, styles, lives
Happiness, stress, tears
Sometimes we lose ourselves trying to find ourselves
When we were ourselves from the start
We were just looking too hard.
Music and radios are still the same
Still playing music and affecting our ways
School never changed, still teaching
Restaurants still feeding, we're still eating
Money still buys everything but happiness
Still causes greed causing unfortunate sadness
The sun is still hot, the rain is still wet, and the snow is still cold.

Things don't change, we do.
We change outfits, styles, shoes,
Hairstyles, personalities, moods,
Expressions, faces, bodies,
We develop, we grow, we shrink, work, fight
Give in, give up, win, lose, cry, laugh, and think
We love, we're lost, heartache
We get sick, we become healed, we see, we touch, we feel
We are rich, poor, we are human
We cause change but…

Things don't change, we do.
Our thoughts, songs, feelings, expressions,
We paint every situation.
We cause every situation.
We live, we die, we kill, we survive
We change
Things stay the same…
We change.

Rock Friend
Victoria Olds
Smyrna High School, Grade 12

Walking along the sidewalk, pockets warming my hands
I take a gander at the pavement, I spot a pile of sand
No reason for it to just sit I say
With the sand I would love to play

Dig, dig, dig, my fingers sink deeply into the dune
I better have fun fast, dinner will be ready soon
Before I go I feel a lump that rubs against my hand
There below the sand pile I've found a small rock friend

Picking him up gently, we walk together towards home
There is no other feeling like having a rock friend to call all your own
I talk to him, whispering my dreams
At school together we learn new things

Rock friend is friendly, friendly, and fun
Although he is silent my heart he has won
He does not mock me, he never makes fun
He listens intently from the start and with no hands to speak of he leaves hand-prints on my heart

First of Many
Christopher Nobile
Smyrna High School, Grade 11

I'm writing to tell a story
Of the dramatic tension of
Competitive swimming

There is no better feeling in
The world than when you step onto
That block. Anxious to show off
Your countless hours of intense
Training.
You hear the cheers of team members and the silence of
Your mind. Preparing yourself for
Your event.
You take your mark. Setting the
Spring in your mind. Screaming of the
Crowd increases then, you start
There is a sudden splash… then silence…
The cold water pierces your body
and as your momentum pushes you
Through the water

Then you take your first
Of many strokes

Look Beside You
Chelsea Nicholson
Smyrna High School, Grade 9

When heartbreak brings you down
And you wonder who's around
To pick you up when your knees hit the ground
Look beside you
Grab the closest hand
Whoever that may be

When memories flood your mind
And you feel you're in a bind
Who will be so kind?
To help you up
Look beside you
Grab the closest hand
Whoever that may be

When you feel alone in your pain
And it seems the world is going insane
Inside you is growing a horrific stain
A stain that will never disappear
Look beside you
Grab the closest hand
Whoever that may be

My Dog
Kelly Day
Smyrna Elementary School, Grade 4

My dog Oskar is so cute.
He sleeps day and night.
He is quite a sight.

My dog Oskar looks like a hotdog you see.
Some might call him a wiener or a sausage link.
He is tan, not pink.

My dog Oskar is my best friend.
Nothing will make me hate him.

Home
Ashley Colemon
Smyrna High School, Grade 9

If home is where the heart is,
then my home is not on this Earth.
My home is in heaven with my Savior
who gave me new birth.

My home is perfect, there is no crying or
sorrow, and no one has to pray for a
better tomorrow.

My heart is in a place where
I can be myself without criticism or scrutiny,
because the people there accept me for <u>me</u>.

There is no pain or struggle, and the best thing of all,
is that I get to spend eternity with my Savior who
looks at my heart, that's all.

Parker Hewitt • Siegel High School • Grade 12

My Selfless Dream
Bailey Carpenter
Smyrna High School, Grade 9

Being on <u>Home Makeover</u> is something I'd like to do
even though it'd be something new.
Sometimes I cry when the family's story is told
since they didn't know what their future would hold.
People who sacrifice
that end up paying the price.
When they don't know which way to go
those of <u>Home Makeover</u> will know.
With times this tough
things can be rough.
So it's time to build
all of those who are willed.
A house full of love
A miracle sent from God above.

Lemon
Brian Williams
Smyrna Elementary School, Grade 5

On the outside you look like a soccer ball.
You feel like a hard sponge.
When I peel you, you sound like an aluminum can being crushed.

Inside you look like a ten piece fraction.
You feel like very bumpy gravel
You smell like a new air freshener
You taste like sour gummy worms

Tell me, my friend, why are you so sour?

The Christmas Miracle
Shelby Jones
LaVergne Middle School, Grade 7

Today was a day, no ordinary day,
It was the day before Santa came, hurray!
The house was decorated with lights and a tree
And the smell, oh the smell, was like heaven to me.
The freshly fallen snow was as white as a cloud
And we were all sleeping without a sound
On this cold, quiet day, a howl broke the silence
We thought it was Santa, here with our presents
We ran to the door, not believing our eyes
We were met by a big surprise
A small dog ran in as we opened the door
And he ran all around, sniffing galore
We gave him warm blankets and water and food
And he lay on the couch in a most sleepy mood
When my mom returned from work, she gave a loud shout
And the dog jumped up and scurried about
"That dog, that dog, what is he doing in here?"
I saw him yesterday and he gave me such a fear!
We pleaded, "But it's Christmas, you gotta let him stay."
"Fine," she said, "but just through Christmas day."
She said, "He needs a bath, he surely does,
He has been hiding under our porch for months."
She picked him up and carried him away
And a Christmas miracle happened that day
He didn't bite, was not even mad
He just looked all pitiful and sad
Although she hadn't wanted to start
During the bath, he won her heart
When the bath was over, she carried him downstairs
It was as if they had always been the perfect pair
He was a tiny, shivering sight
And she said to us in awe, "He didn't try to bite!"
From that moment on, we were bonded at the soul
And my mom wouldn't have cared if Santa only brought coal
Now, it's plain to see, he didn't leave
Not even five years after that first Christmas Eve!
My mom named him Wizzer, a funny name I agree,
But she named him that cause he liked to pee
Now without this dog, our family would surely die
Even gone one day, we would cry
He was the greatest gift we got that day,
A gift for which we didn't have to pay
He makes my mom happy, he comes when she calls

He fills up her heart, every bit of it, all
This is why I must say
He is our Christmas miracle to this day!

Best Friends Forever
Hayden Petty
Thurman Francis Arts Academy, Grade 2

Best friends forever,
I really like you.
We've been friends forever,
I don't want to stop now.
We get in trouble but…
All I want to do is be with you.
Even though we are not in the same class,
We are still best friends forever.

Quiggly
Andy King
Thurman Francis Arts Academy, Grade 2

Three years ago I got a dog with big ears.
Although he is short
He is bigger than a wart.
A lady brought him to us
And she didn't ride a bus.
We named him Quiggly,
And he is still wiggly.
He is a Wheaton Terrier
And is too big for a carrier.
He's at home right now
Doing nothing because he is lazy.

Basketball
Mack Ferrell
Thurman Francis Arts Academy, Grade 7

        This is a dream, this is hope,
        This is a chance, for me to hold.
        This is a team, these are some friends,
        Who never quit, until the end.
        This is a team, just chasing a dream,
        Always trying to be the best they can be.
        This is me, hitting a three
        Becoming known, from sea to sea.
        They shout my name as I come out,
        Onto the court, my teammates around.
        Beside me my coach, as I hear him shout,
        "This is the day, make me proud!"
        Sound of the whistle, feel of the ball,
        I feel like a king, who will never fall.
        We end with a win, it was nasty,
        They looked like my grandmother, dear old McPatsy.
        This is a dream, this is hope,
        This is a chance, for me to hold.

Handprints on My Heart
Chris Smith
Thurman Francis Arts Academy, Grade 6

Handprints on my heart
It's something you might need
They're from loved ones and family
It helps you to plant the seed.

Your heart is what carries
Love of all kinds
From the softest of people
To the most serious of minds.

You can do something
To help do your part
To help put the handprints
On everybody's heart.

Handprints on My Heart
Cassidy Conard
Thurman Francis Arts Academy, Grade 7

Handprints on my heart,
They're his I know it's true.
The only problem is,
He doesn't know it too.

He holds it every day.
He has it everywhere he goes.
I say he holds my heart
Even though he doesn't know.

Life may be tough,
But he makes it all worthwhile
With his beautiful eyes
And his dazzling smile.

I'm standing in the background
Watching him every day
As he carries around my heart
And doesn't throw it away.

When asked how he feels,
He simply shakes his head
But I know that deep down
There is a better feeling than dread.

Relationships may end,
Others will drift apart,
But we will be forever
Because of his handprints on my heart.

Handprints on My Heart
Kennedy Wallace
Thurman Francis Arts Academy, Grade 4

Fairest friends
Riding bikes and shopping
I love friends
Excellent times and memories
Never rude remarks or violence
Dreaming together at slumber parties
Shopping is what we do best together

The Dream for Me
Kristen Hunsicker
Thurman Francis Arts Academy, Grade 7

The sand washes upon my feet
Seashells appear as waves come and go
Many fun activities to do in the heat
I waste my energy till there is nothing to do
An exciting day at the beach is a perfect day

A weekend at the ballpark
Many exciting games are played
Waiting under shady trees against the bark
Until my time to shine arrives
As excitement is building, a dream is forming

Another day comes and goes just like that
Waiting to find my niche
I try searching every day
But when I finally find it
My dream will be complete

O, what a wonderful day that will be!

I Want to Be
Sydney Henn
Thurman Francis Arts Academy, Grade 8

I want to be an astronaut
No, I take that back
I want to be a doctor
Or an athlete running track
I could profess a college course
Or be a sniper in the army
Or a busy party planner
Throwing one heck of a party
It would be nice to be a dentist
Making teeth all nice and white,
Or I would like to be a deckhand
Fighting waves all through the night
I could always be a teacher,
Oh, no, that wouldn't do
I couldn't stand tons of kids
Always crowding you
How about an explorer?
Traveling places far and near
Or a sweet librarian saying,
"Please quiet down, my dear."
I could be a confident lawyer,
Defender, and persuader
A singer, an artist,
Or a graceful figure skater
On second thought,
Forget it.
I'll wait until high school
Then I'll see
Just what wondrous journey
God has in store for me.

Handprints on My Heart
Delaney Mitchell
Smyrna Primary School, Grade 1

Dear Abby,
    Do you love uthr people? Yes, I do! Then, you shod play with the people that you love. Abby, do you love me, too? Yes, I do!

Sincerley,
Delaney

Someone Like Me
Sydney Dodd
Thurman Francis Arts Academy, Grade 4

I dream of a person
Who stands alone like me
They would be able to see and breathe
And be all they could be
Who is on their own
All by themselves
They wouldn't be like anyone else
They would love to play
And never be afraid
They would stand up for themselves
And be able to say
"Thank you for this wonderful day."

Dream of a Better World
Lindsay Bouldin
Thurman Francis Arts Academy, Grade 4

When you look at the world,
There is a lot of pollution.
Fighting and killing
It seems like there is no solution

Dream of a better world
With no guns or knives
Not even one sword.
There is always life.

Lions and tigers are gentle like sheep
Playing with children
Who are piled like a trash heap
Wearing big grins.

When you make it seem happy,
It will feel so right,
It will make you slaphappy!
Imagine living in a paradise.

Being in a better world,
Is the best place you could be.
Try to imagine,
And you can see.
Dream of a better world.

I Don't Know
Grace Scruggs
Smyrna West Alternative School, Grade 7

She means a lot to me
Only if she understood.
I want to tell her, but only if I could.
What will she say, or what will she do?
I don't know, but I tried so hard,
I know I did the best I could.

One Chance
Kane Wilkerson
Smyrna West Alternative School, Grade 9

I've learned my lesson.
I want to go home.
Trouble is no fun,
Just let me go.

Give me a chance.
Just once more.

I will make it last.
Not like before.

Lily
Alexia Halford
Walter Hill Elementary School, Grade 2

    I miss my dog Lily. Though she was fat and lazy, she was playful and full of love. Lily enjoyed bath time, and she loved to hide her bones in our clothes. She loved her treats, and boy did she love to eat! She was very sweet. I will always miss her.

Labels
Dominique Woodard
Smyrna West Alternative School, Grade 10

Have you ever been labeled?

Well you're one of the lucky ones.

Jock
Goth
Emo
Flirt
Bad boy
Criminal

I'm none of those.
I'm just me.

People think labels describe them
In reality they're just a crutch

Next time someone labels you, say
No.
You're wrong.
I'm just me.

Fall
Kailey Butler
Smyrna Primary School, Grade 5

Fall
Cool, Wet
Leaves, Weather, Trees
Dying, Raking, Swimming, Diving
Pools, Kids, Fireworks
Hot, Dry
Summer

School Is Fun
Annabelle Diefenbaugh
Smyrna Primary School, Grade 2

School is fun. We do math and we read. I like to read. It is fun. I like to play with my friend Hailey and Colby. They like to play with me, too. I love school and I always will.

Levi
Ethan Day
Smyrna Primary School, Grade 1

My dog's name is Levi. He is a black and white Boston Terrier, and he licks my face a lot. Levi likes to chase me around the yard. At night we sleep for twelve hours.

My Hamster
Shaylee Ezell
Smyrna Primary School, Grade 1

My hamster is quite funny because she dances. She likes to climb up the cage to get treats, then she hides from me in the mulch and dances.

My Teacher
Vivian Seay
Smyrna Primary School, Grade 1

Ms. Boe is important to me, because she is my teacher. She teaches me everything. She can do important, neat stuff to help me be a great doctor when I grow up.

Handprints on My Heart
Claire Cahoon
Siegel Middle School, Grade 8

One sandcastle on a massive beach,
Adults think school is just to teach
That we're here to know two and two equals four,
But the students know better, the students know more.
What we do here is the rest of our life,
If we pass up the chances, we're just doomed to strife.
For school is society—only small-scale,
And how we do here, is how we do there.

So whether it's drama or football or band,
What you do now is the world in your hands.
For if you can learn what you're good at or like,
You can find a career, not job you dislike.
Though grown-ups may say "Do your work, don't' explore!"
The students know better, the students know more.
So look at the people that you sit by now
And know that one day, somewhere, somehow,
They could change your life forever.

Widgets
Christine Choo
Siegel High School, Grade 12

You were the beacon of light at my dire crossroad
Guiding me not through orders or speech,
But through care and acts of faith.
You met me at a very interesting time in my life;
I was freshly recovering from the skewed delusion that had consumed me
the preceding year.
Always a victim of indecisiveness,
I did not know if, or how, to change.
But like a religious epiphany,
It was by your divine grace that I was transformed.
You believed in me,
And little by little that began to soften my rough edges.
You say you saw a spark in me,
An undeniable potential.
Unknowing to you, you were the first person to truly believe in me.
You were the catalyst in my life that fueled a change in my attitude.
I no longer belittled my own abilities in the fear of failure.
A father figure and teacher in every aspect of the word,
You have taught me to live a life I can take pride in,
Taught me to exert all my energies in what I am passionate about,
And taught me to always pay it forward.
Your overwhelming lesson is love,
And for that, I thank you.

Identical
Lauren Pearson
Siegel High School, Grade 10

As I look out at the dark world in front of me, I see my reflection in the window and see the same darkness. The fire in my eyes has been put out. I can't take my eyes away from the reflection…what have I let myself become? A strong person is like a waterfall, they make their own paths. But we're too sick to let this world go, and too scared to let this darkness die. There's the edge of the universe and the breath is sucked out of our lungs and we fall to the ground. This reflection is the same as everyone else's. It's my own and billions of others. I've fallen victim to this world more times than I can fathom, and obviously, so have you. I'm the dead rising from the open grave, the failure; I am the demon and the prophet. My steps have taken the world's atmosphere and I've been blind to all I've seen. I've lost every bit of time I had left, and here I am, billions as one, staring at my reflection, wondering where the time has gone.

Who?
Jacob Schultz
Siegel High School, Grade 9

Who guarded over me in the womb?
Who watched over my birth?
Who led my parents to my baptism,
Never doubting my worth?
Who forgives and forgets?
Who leads me through life?
Through good times and bad,
Through calm and through strife.
Who lives in my heart,
Body, mind, and soul?
Who fills me with joy,
When my life gets so dull?
Who died for me once,
And would do it again?
The ultimate role model,
Teacher, and friend.
Who is there on my journey,
Was there from the start?
It was You, Jesus Christ,
Who left handprints on my heart.

Touch Every Heart with Love
Nausheen Qureshi
Siegel High School, Grade 9

Many prints are left on the sand,
By dawn most have been washed away,
Only but a few are etched in time itself,
Reminders to all of happier days,
Of loved ones and their sweet words,
So why waste what little you have to be erased?
Try,
Try your hardest,
To leave a mark,
A mark so strong that it can never be taken by the tide,
A symbol of true love,
A symbol of hope,
Because in the end,
Only you can leave a handprint on every heart you touch,
One that you know will last an eternity,
One that will fuel them with the strength they need,
With the courage and the valor,
To live in this world.

Flying
Ellen Allbritten
Siegel High School, Grade 10

    I am flying, I say. My legs are brushing against the scratchy trees that feel like sandpaper. My hair is slapping my face and getting into my mouth and sticking to my lip gloss like a sticker. My flip flops are hanging on to the very edge of my toes, teasing and taunting me, telling me they are getting ready to jump off my feet. My hands are burning from the rough rope that rubs against my hands like the tags that make me itch from the inside of the back of my shirt. The hairs on my arms are threatening to jump off, they are raised so high.
    One tiny black rope is the only thing keeping me from plummeting to my death in the backyard. One rope is all that I am trusting to not let me fall like one of those Barbie dolls that we threw from the deck just to see where they would land. One of the Barbies actually got stuck in a tree, floating there for hours like a dead fish at the top of the tank.
    I am a butterfly, one of those pretty purple ones that we only see once or twice a year in the summer. I am fearless, a shark among a tank of teeny, immature goldfish. My happiness is soaring as the houses get far away, then closer, far away, then closer. My smile is about to jump off my face.
    Then the ground returns. It welcomes me back with a warm hug. A hug almost as big as the one my dad gave me when he returned home from Afghanistan after being gone for six months. I step off the teal swing that is shaped like a disc with a black rope attached to the middle and tied at the bottom. I smile, and the rush of adrenaline flashes in my brain like a tattoo.

Signs of Winter
Megan Meadow
Siegel Middle School, Grade 7

Drinking hot chocolate by the fire
And snow falling is what I desire
I picture my family singing together
Even if we were having bad weather
Nothing can spoil this perfect season
Not even the Grinch should have a reason
As cold winds sting my skin
I now know that winter will soon begin.

Simply Rain

Brian Allen
Siegel High School, Grade 11

In a rural town of a western state,
In a desert where it hadn't rained of late,
Something began to approach, oh so rare
An ominous gray cloud filled the air.

At their windows, kids covered in dust
Desired nothing but the rain for which they lust.
Day after day parched by the unrelenting sun,
They waited in anticipation of the wet, wild fun.

Huzzah! The raindrops began to pour,
And jubilant kids ran out their door.
They jumped around with arms in the air;
The rain had come . . . as if answering a prayer.

The rain intensified and water accrued;
By no means, was their laughter subdued.
They skipped and jumped; they shouted and screamed.
A day for love, life, and laughter – it was deemed.

Taking advantage of the obscured sun,
The parents decided to witness the fun.
Watching the games, they took great delight;
Their kids' laughter was such a welcome sight.

After a couple of joyous hours passed,
The torrential rain came to an end at last.
Suddenly, a virtually unknown image appeared:
A magnificent rainbow; the children all cheered.

The awe-struck kids gawked at the sight
Of the beautifully arranged streaks of light.
Such a simple thing, the coming of the rain,
But the life, love, and laughter would long remain.

Home Is Where the Heart Is
Caroline Daws
Siegel High School, Grade 11

I remember sitting in a secret place, hiding from the world.
A place to open my mind, but close it to the worries of life.
That place is home.
My home is not a house, it does not have parents,
and my home doesn't have home-cooked meals.
My home is not luxurious, and it is not a material paradise.
But my home has heart.
My home has sunsets so alluring they are magnificently reflected in your eyes,
morphing from blue to pink, then a deep, warm orange.
My home has a library with endless rows of books, covers hugging pages.
My home has rooms upon rooms of smiles like
sunshine peeking out from behind a rain cloud.
Home sees beautiful words from beautiful minds
penned onto pristine paper.
My home rings with the sound of united voices
wandering across peaceful melodies.
Home is brushed with the whispers of a thousand distant winds,
echoed in soft leaves.
My home is a short-lived neverland, where time and space have
no limits, no control.
My home is never unkind, never fearful, and never lonely.
My home is filled with friends so close, family feels distant.
My home is people,
it is laughter, emotions, it is memories.
Home,
is where the heart is.

Outside
Graham Bateman
Walter Hill Elementary School, Grade 2

The sky is bright,
Soon it will be night.
The day is hot.
I'm looking for a cool spot.
So I run like a bull
And jump into a pool.

On a Cold Winter Day
Savannah Lee
Siegel Middle School, Grade 7

When the sun rises on a cold winter day
I put on snuggly warm clothes
And go outside and play
As I go down a big hill on my sleigh
I sing merrily, "I'm having a great day!"

I smile and I laugh as I join my friends
And I think to myself, I hope this day never ends!
The warmth of the sun
Melts the snow, so it packs just right
Then we have a big snowball fight.

The sun starts to go down
And we start to tire
Then we relax by the big open fire
I close my eyes with much content
Remembering the enjoyment
Of a sunrise on a cold winter day.

They Need Our Help
Aran Moran
Siegel Middle School, Grade 7

She raised her fist and screamed at him
He was quivering, defenseless, innocent
Nowhere to run; no way to escape
He cowered on his short leash
She brought her fist down hard and fast
With full force, smashing it into his ribs
Confused he looked up at her with big sad eyes
Crying out in pain, he looked at her
As if to ask her why
I witnessed this cruelty
Anger and nausea overtook me
I wanted to save him
I wanted her to feel his humiliation, his fear, his pain
God's innocent creatures need our protection
Animal abuse needs to stop now!

Fathers
Christopher Haley
Siegel Middle School, Grade 6

Fathers, what are they like? I wish I knew. Gregory Haley is my birth father, but I don't know him. I know what he looks like, but I don't know him. I went to live with my grandmother when I was one month old. My sister came with me; she was seventeen months old. When I was two, my sister and I were adopted and my grandmother became our mother.

For a long time I didn't really think about fathers. I hadn't one, and I wasn't very curious about them. As I got older, I started to notice them, but I didn't really think about what it would be like to have one in my life until the spring of 2008 when I played baseball. I noticed many dads cheering for their sons at practice games and at all of the real games. I noticed how they treated their sons, and how they helped them practice. I watched the coach with his son as well, and noticed how he helped each of us learn the rules about baseball. Baseball was a lot of fun. It would have been nice to share that with a father.

Although I don't know my father, I'd still like to get to know him. I want to know what he likes to do and what interests him. Does he like sports? If he does like sports, I wonder what kind of sports he likes most of all – football, baseball, or basketball? I think I might be more interested in playing sports if I had had a dad I could have practiced with.

Dads can also teach sons about other things like fixing bikes, painting, camping, hiking, and many other activities. I miss not having a dad. I think I would really like to know my dad. Dads are important. I wish……

My Best Friend
Ashley Gray
Siegel Middle School, Grade 7

Carter Marie
Is more than a best friend to me,
Much more than anyone else could be.
I know that she will always be there,
In the good times and the bad,
Even if I'm happy or sad.
We do most everything together,
And that will stay like that forever.
We stay up late at night,
Using sticks to get the bugs out of her light.
We also get into lots of fights.
We argue about every little thing,
And neither one of us knows how to sing.
She will always have a special place in my heart,
We can never ever stay apart!

Feelings of My Heart
Rodolfo Danny Martinez
Roy Waldron Elementary School, Grade 4

Mom cooks dinner when I get back from school
      And I feel joyful!
My dad helps me with my homework
      And I feel cheerful!
My sister plays with me
      And I feel overjoyed!
My friends help me with things like skating on my skateboard
      And I feel glad!
My mom and dad came to America for me
      And I feel loved!
My choir practices are fun
      And I feel thankful!
Stray dogs play with me almost every day
      And I feel elated!

I Wonder
Adrian Garcia
Roy Waldron Elementary School, Grade 5

I wonder
  If I will pass the fifth grade
I wonder
  If I will handle life on my own
I wonder
  If I will have a good career
I wonder
  If I am going to meet some good friends along my life's journey
I wonder
  If my friends will remember me as I grow old
I wonder
  If I will get a chance to see the White House
I wonder
  If I will achieve my goals
I wonder
  If I am going to meet the love of my life
I wonder
  If I will **live** until I die

My Best Friend
Madison Nippers
Rockvale Elementary School, Grade 5

When I first came to Rockvale Elementary, I was so frightened. But in third grade I met Samantha. Samantha and I have been friends ever since – not one fight or fuss. Almost every weekend, either I go to her house or she comes to mine. Samantha has always stood up for me, and I have stood up for her. Friends are like a dog and a flea, they stick together and stay together just like Samantha and I. We are like sisters. Everyone should have a good friend like Samantha. This is what friendship is about. I hope you find a friend like Samantha, too.

My First Recital
Kaylee Flores
Rockvale Elementary School, Grade 5

I was nervous. I wasn't sure what the steps were. I was only four. Was it shuffle-step, ball change, or toe, heel, ball change? The lights went out.

My tap class's dance was next. There were so many steps that I forgot. My class started to walk on the stage, so I followed them while I breathed in the sweet smelling smoke. I tried to remember everything Mrs. Angela, my tap teacher, taught me in the past year. But the music started.

The song "Boogie Baby," started, and I needed to start dancing. I had no idea what I was supposed to do! My family always told me not to look at the other people because they could be wrong. But this time, I had no choice. I started to turn my head to see what my classmates were doing, but then my feet just started moving. It felt like I wasn't doing anything! I started to dance by myself just doing what my feet do without looking at other people!

Finally, the dance was over. I only remember hearing applause and my family cheering for me and waving the phone at me. Then I knew I had done a good job.

Bugs
Grace Scivicque
Christiana Elementary School, Grade 1

I like bugs. They are terrific. Bugs fly, bugs hop, and bugs crawl. That is a lot. That is cool! I love bugs. Sometimes bugs are really soft. A flea itches and it jumps really high! I have great times with bugs. All bugs are special. Some bugs make clicking and buzzing noises. I love bugs in different shapes and sizes. When I hold bugs they freak me out because they touch my hand and it feels prickly. I still like bugs anyway.

Happy Halloween
Alyssa Rhinehart
Christiana Elementary School, Grade 1

Once upon a time there was a black cat named Halloween. Halloween was always her favorite day of the year. She liked watching the glowing jack-o-lanterns and following the trick-or-treaters. They would scratch her ears and give her treats. She can't wait until next year.

Summer Makes Me Happy
Dallen Garrett
Christiana Elementary School, Grade 2

Summer makes me happy because my Dad takes me fishing. We catch the fish and then we let them go. We take some of the fish home and cook them. They taste yummy! In the summer I love fishing. Summer makes me happy.

My Cat Tigger
Malayna Wacaster
Christiana Elementary School, Grade 4

I have had Tigger since I was a little girl around two years old. He stayed at my dad's house, because my mom doesn't like cats at all. I did not have any friends around except Tigger. Without him I felt so lonely. Every night when I was little, I got scared. So, I would go into the living room and bring him in, and he would sleep at the bottom of my bed. I was happy when he was around. He was my favorite cat ever.

Then, not too long ago, my dad got kicked out of his house, because he did not have enough money to pay the bills. When he left, he had to live with my grandma until he could find a house. When he moved there, Tigger ran away. He did not know what else to do. We looked everywhere and couldn't find him. I would be so glad if I could find him, because he is the best.

Kindergarten
Noah McAlister
Christiana Elementary School, Kindergarten

Kindergarten is great because ist BIG.

Genuine Patriot
Megan Taylor
Christiana Elementary School, Grade 5

If you have never honored a veteran on Veterans' Day, you should give it a go. I had always thought of this holiday as a boring, pointless one until 1999. That was when my dad joined the U.S. Army. I was nine when he joined. I never wanted him to go, but he was a genuine patriot. From then on, Veterans' Day has meant a lot to me.

Dad was a good man. He wasn't perfect, but almost. He was a good soldier always following the general's orders. How he longed to be a general! He would always write to me saying with every step he took in another country, with every bullet he fired at an enemy, he was getting closer to achieving his goal. He only spoke up when the general's orders were unpatriotic. He didn't even speak up when the commands were sure to kill him. He was the best.

My life went on for two years like that. I received a letter every Saturday from him, each one reminding me of what a good patriot he was. I was never worried for him; it seemed as if he could never die. I only started to worry when I saw the letter one Saturday. Most people wouldn't be afraid, but I was. The letter said he was flying home. At first I thought I was horrible for not wanting this, but the simple fact was: he was safe in another country; he wasn't safe on a plane. Terrorists were always crashing planes on purpose. He was coming home on Tuesday, September 11.

Mom planned a huge Welcome Home parade and party for all of the soldiers that were coming home. Everybody in the state of New York was invited, with a few out-of-state friends and family. Everyone was excited, but I think I was the most ecstatic. Daddy was coming home!

On September 11, I got up before the crack of dawn. I was surprised to see Mom up, ready to go. She must have not gotten any sleep like me. Since it was only two-thirty, we turned on the news. When I saw the breaking news flash, all my worry came back to me. Three terrorists were caught yesterday, and more were expected today. What if Dad were on a plane that had a terrorist on it?

I forgot all my worries when we got to the parade. It was in front of the Twin Towers. People were all over the street, dressed in red, white, and blue. We were all waiting for the planes to fly overhead and drop off the homecoming soldiers.

The next thing that happened was a horrifying event. We started to hear the buzzing of the jet engines coming closer. It didn't turn out as we all thought it would. Suddenly, the Twin Towers blew up in a cloud of smoke. They burst into fames and then collapsed. From then on, it was all a blur.

When I woke up, I was in the Intensive Care Center at the hospital. It was two weeks after the Twin Towers were destroyed. The doctors said I was lucky to be alive. When I was fully awake, I asked where my mom was. They said she was checking both of us out of the hospital.

Suddenly, I sat straight up in bed. "Where's Dad!?!" I practically yelled.

One of the doctors stared at me, but then he asked, "Was he a soldier coming home on a plane?"

"Yes!" I cried, worrying more and more about my dad.

"There's no easy way to say this," the doctor started. I started to sob. "All the passengers on the planes... they died."

"No!" I screamed. "Dad couldn't have! He doesn't deserve it! He didn't do anything wrong!"

"Honey, NODODY deserved to die on the planes but the terrorists," Mom said as she walked in the door. I jumped out of bed.

"Mommy! Why didn't Dad stay in Iraq? Why did he get on that stupid plane?" I regretted blaming it on Dad. How could he be at fault when all he wanted was to come see Mom and me? I started to sob harder as I embraced Mom.

I remembered that Dad was in a better place now. He was in heaven. I hoped he was having a good time. I silently told God that he was a great man. I couldn't wait to see him.

Two months after the Twin Tower incident, it was Veteran's Day. I didn't wear my usual red, white, and blue outfit. I wore my outfit that I hated, but Dad loved. I hoped he was watching as we took part in the Veterans' Day Parade. Everyone had to say one veteran's name. I said Bobby Heart, the most genuine patriot.

A Storybook
Peyton Fogle
Christiana Elementary School, Grade 3

I have heard a story that has touched my heart and it the called "A Storybook." It is called "A Storybook" because it has all kinds of stories. And my mom read it to me all the time when I was little. I loved that book very much. My mom now reads it to my brothers Maddox and Owen. So when my mom reads to me, that really touches my heart and my brothers' hearts, but mostly me.

Things That Make Me Happy
Alexis Crank
Christiana Elementary School, Grade 2

I like many things. I like to play with my family because it makes me happy. Going to school makes me very happy. I like to see my teacher and all of my friends. Climbing trees and looking down from far up makes my heart fill with joy and puts a smile on my face. I love life!

Fall Leaves
Katie King
Christiana Elementary School, Grade 4

The moon is shining,
The stars are bright,
Everything is settled
On this beautiful night.

The moon is white,
The stars are yellow,
These things provide light
For the next fellow.

The wind starts to blow,
The trees start to shake,
The leaves fall down
Into the lake.

The night is going to cease.
The sun will rise,
I will awake
And there is a surprise.

The morning has started.
It is a beginning of a new day.
I hope everything is good,
While I'm away.

Thank You
Tionne Emmons
Christiana Elementary School, Grade 3

      I want to thank all the Veterans for letting the United States be free. Thanks for being in the Air Force, Navy, Marines, Coast Guard, and Army. You have given your life for our freedom. Thank you a lot. You make a handprint on our hearts. We have schools, houses, freedom, and veterans.

This Is What Makes Me Happy
Samara Simmons
Christiana Elementary School, Grade 2

Let me tell you what makes me happy. My mom and daddy make me very happy. They take care of me and love me. My friends make me happy. They are nice and sweet. That's what makes me happy.

I Like to
Collin Dye
Christiana Elementary School, Kindergarten

I like to fotBol with my friends.

Marines
Caleb Lay
Christiana Elementary School, Grade 5

Making our country free.
Always marching for our freedom.
Right and just.
Inspiring children around the world.
Not stopping to rest.
Eager to do what's right.
Soldiers who believe in freedom.

Sherman
Ridge Sessions
Walter Hill Elementary School, Grade 2

Sherman
Playful, orange, fat
He likes to play with string.
Sometimes at night,
He likes to sing!
Meow, meow, meow
I love my cat!

Maggie
Rachel Foster
Christiana Elementary School, Grade 3

One night when I was listening to my dad read <u>Harry Potter and the Chamber of Secrets</u>. My cat Maggie jumped on my bed, found a place on me, and lay down and listened with me.

She was so cute with her pointy ears sticking up listening with me. When my dad left, Maggie followed him. My mom came in to read my sister and me a story, say goodnight, and then she left. Maggie came in again, jumped on my bed, and found a spot to lie down beside me. She rested for a bit and left.

The next morning, Maggie came to the breakfast table, meowed, and came to me. I petted her and she left again.

I love my cat Maggie. She is my best friend.

My Hope for Soccer
Samantha White
Wilson Elementary School, Grade 5

Soccer is my passion,
It is a pure obsession.
I play basketball too,
But soccer makes it through.
I like making the ball roll,
I could even get a goal.
I love offense,
It just makes sense.
I want to be a professional,
That just sounds sensational.
Soccer is my passion,
It is a pure obsession.

My Favorite Place
Mattie Webb
Wilson Elementary School, Grade 1

My favorite place in my life is church. I like it because you learn about God and Jesus. They are the best people I love.

Softball
Hailey Lopez
Brown's Chapel Elementary School, Grade 5

So my place to be!
Over the fence is a homerun!
Fast pitchers!
Tough players.
Ball is *not* soft!
All around the world people play it.
Lots of cheering!
Lots of fun!

Thanksgiving
Kaitlyn Estes
Brown's Chapel Elementary School, Grade 5

I love the smell of turkey being cooked, and the smell of chocolate pie.
I can taste the mashed potatoes and gravy warm in my mouth, and the cold chocolate pie.
I can hear my family laughing and playing. I can even hear my sister giggling.
I can see the huge turkey. I can see my brother covered in pie, too.
I feel all the love from my family.
I feel the autumn breeze.

My Pet Giraffe
Faith Buck
Brown's Chapel Elementary School, Grade 3

I have a pet giraffe. He loves to play catch. I love him so much, because he helps me reach stuff! He is my best friend in the world. I look at him out my window every night and sometimes he comes to my bedroom and licks me. It's fun to ride him. He's the best in the world!!!!!!

A Boy's Journey to Fly
Trevor Gaines
Lascassas Elementary School, Grade 6

He was about 5'3" with long blonde hair and a nice, smooth complexion. He lived in the diminutive town of Walter Hill, TN. His life long dream was to fly an airplane. This boy's name was Brian Smith.

Brian loved airplanes. Attenuated planes, state-of-the-art planes, hefty planes, miniature planes, no matter what it looked like, he loved them. His favorite one was the voluminous Airbus A380, a double-deck, wide-body, four-engine airliner. It was the largest passenger airliner in the world.

He really wanted to go to flight school so he could become a pilot. But he only had $20. To go to flight school, he needed to have $4,460. He didn't have that much money. He still needed $4,440, so he decided to get a neighborhood job.

He was an animal lover, so he decided to be a pet sitter. His first job was for a little old lady named Erma Johanson. She had a petite, black Boston terrier.

"Now you take care of my sweet little Pookie-kins, young man," Ms. Johanson affirmed.

"Don't worry, Ms. Johanson. I will make sure your Pookie-kins is properly pampered." Brian replied.

As soon as she left to get her car fixed, Brian took Pookie-kins in the house to feed her. But when he set her down, she ran out the doggie door in the front door. "Pookie-kins!" Brian yelled. "Come back! What is Ms. Johanson going to do?"

Brian sped out the door and looked for her. He soon found her by the creek three blocks away. "Pookie-kins, stop!!!" Brian bellowed. He tried running after her but she slipped when a car raced by. Brian leaped in after her. He then pulled her to the surface. On the way back home, Brian noticed a cut right behind her front left leg. *Oh come on,* he thought.

When he walked through the door, there Ms. Johanson was sitting in her chair. "Ms. Johanson, I can explain." But she lay still, eyes closed. "Ms. Johanson? Oh, no!" He picked up the phone. He called 911. The operator said, "What's your emergency?"

Brian yelped into the phone, "I don't think my friend Erma Johanson is breathing!!!"

"Hang on, we'll be right there," the operator said.

"OK," Brian said.

The paramedics picked her up and took her to the hospital. He got on his bike and rode to the hospital. She was at StoneCrest Medical Center. When he walked into Ms. Johanson's room, she said, "Thanks for saving my life, Brian, and my dog's life. I think you deserve this." She handed him an envelope. Inside was $4,440.

"Whoa!" Brian screamed. "What's this for?"

Ms. Johanson replied, "$4,000 for saving my life, $400 for saving my dog's life, and $40 since it was your birthday a week ago."

"Thanks," Brian said, "this is just the amount I need for school."

"I know, flight school."

Brian is now the co-pilot for the 7th Airbus A380 because of Ms. Johanson's generous reward. He is in love with his job and his friend thinks that he will never quit his job because he loves it so much. If it weren't for Ms. Erma Johanson, Brian would not be where he is today.

My Dog Duke
Mallory Mosier
Blackman Elementary School, Grade 5

When I saw him run to me
I smiled and laughed.
Trying to think about the past
When I've always wanted a dog
Just like Duke.

When he was a puppy
He went in the house and sat on the couch.
He sat on my lap, taking lots of naps.
Soon he was too big to play outside
So we gave him his own room in the garage.
With a fan blowing in his face to keep him cool
And a heater in the winter to keep him warm.

He's now five years old
With plenty of room to play in the yard.
Loves to go on walks, then hits the hay
In his place where he calls home.

My dog Duke

The Train Museum
Josiah Fulk
Blackman Elementary School, Grade 1

My heart is happy when I go to the train museum. This makes me happy because I like to look at the train. It is a blast.

Army Soldiers
Taylor Gilpin
Blackman Elementary School, Grade 5

Do you think life is cool?
In Iraq, it's just plain cruel.
There are soldiers risking their lives.
Getting stabbed with very sharp knives.
Do you think you're really tough?
A life for a soldier is very rough.
So be thankful for the American ways.
And also be thankful for the 50 states.

Fourth of July
Allison Haeker
Blackman Elementary School, Grade 4

Fireworks and flames high in the sky,
Our relatives come and stop by.
USA, we celebrate you this day.
Run, run look up in the sky,
There they go flying high.
How happy am I.

Oh, how beautiful the sky looks,
Fireworks remind me of our freedom.

Just look and you will find the beauty,
Up in the sky as high as they fly.
Listen, listen and you will hear liberty,
Year, after year it becomes more clear.

Thanksgiving
Nathan Farrington
Blackman Elementary School, Grade 4

Thanksgiving is here!
Haul in all the food,
And give thanks for all we have.
Next, tell all your
Kinfolks the exciting things that happened
Since you last met.
Greet all the unknown people,
It's finally time to eat!
Vegetables, ugh!
I only want turkey.
Now I'm stuffed,
Going to take a nap.

Thanksgiving
Kendall Hughes
Blackman Elementary School, Grade 4

Turkeys in the field, turkeys on the run,
Harvest time is here in 1621.
Autumn has arrived, the trees are turning yellow,
Now gather up the food, with our Indian fellow
Kindly prepare a feast. Cooking can be fun.
Say a blessing and thank our God for what he has done.
Green beans, bread, peas, and mashed potatoes,
Indians even brought their corn and tomatoes.
Vegetables are fine, but I bet they liked the pie.
Imagine all this food, enough to make you sigh.
Now what will Thanksgiving be like in 2009,
Grandma says I have to keep this tradition and somehow make it mine.

Art
Caton Taylor
Blackman Elementary School, Grade 1

I want to be an artist.
I love to paint.
Art is really, really, really fun!

Christmas
Ashlyn Hargrove
Blackman Elementary School, Grade 4

Crowds are shopping,
Halls are hopping.
Ringing bells,
I'm not stopping.
Sugar cookie smells,
Time for holiday tales.
My wish list is sent,
All my money is spent.
Shh, it's time for Santa.

My Triathalon
Tyler Nelson
Blackman Elementary School, Grade 5

Swim, bike, run
These all are very fun
Especially done one by one
Lit up by the morning sun.

Swimming's not my strongest skill
It feels like I'm going uphill.

Biking I really like to do
I pedaled hard and flew, flew, flew.

Running always comes last
But when I run, I have a blast.

Basketball

Sabrea James
Blackman Middle School, Grade 7

Basketball is a sport that I really like to do for fun.
It's also a very tiring sport because you have to run.
You have three seconds in the middle.
Or else you can dribble.
Basketball is very playful,
But it can also be very hurtful.

I like basketball because it makes me happy.
It's also not that sappy.
You have to shoot the ball to make a goal,
You can't rush the ball it has to come from the soul
In basketball you can use your hands,
But you can't use your feet.
You have to control your anger you can't get mad
Sometimes when you lose you get sad.

In basketball there are different positions,
I played a position called point guard.
It's where you dribble down the court.
When you dribble you have to be careful.
Basketball is very shameful.
When you win a game you say,
Hip-hip hooray
You can foul each other but not on purpose.
If you do then it will be the other teams' ball.
That's the reason I like to play basketball.

My Hopes and Dreams of Motorcross Mornings
Bradley Carrithers
Blackman Middle School, Grade 7

In the early morning still black as coal
As the families and friends scramble to get everything prepared
Five o'clock
The sound of the sprinklers wetting the clay-colored dirt.
The mood in the air and smiles from children
Smells of race fuel and half-smoked cigarettes
Flyers, papers, and wristbands among the crowd
Finely tuned machines on two wheels
The roar of forty kids to the first turn
Worried and excited faces behind gates
As tired and muddy eyes come off the track
Thrills and chills from every soul
Where winners are made.

Life Lesson
Bryan Daley
Smyrna West Alternative School, Grade 11

I realize I can't do it on my own
That I need some help.
Looking at my cards
I'll play the hand that I was dealt.
But I take a look at my life
And realize there is nothing left.
Nobody can change me
I've got to change myself.

So for the good of others
I have got to demonstrate
That what you get
Comes from the
Choices you make.

So I must try my best
To get my life straight!

Stop messing up
And stop making those mistakes!

I've got to put my head on right
And make my life great!

Barfield Elementary School
Karen Myers
Laurie Watts

Blackman Elementary School
Wendy Buchanan
Jenna Burke
Kimberly Christopher
Ashley Foster
Rachel Fraser
LaJae Hayes
Kelly Henry
Annette Holloway
Lynn Kennedy
Julie Kirin
Tisonya Maston
Ray Ann McCord
Pam Morgan
Jennifer Navarre
Grayson Rose
Krissa Seifert
Wendy Spivey
Marcella Watts
Brigid Whitaker
Connie Wiel
Mary C. Wilkerson
April Williams
Fannie Williams

Blackman High School
Beth Sinclair
Ruth Anna Thomason

Blackman Middle School
Paige Barber
Leigh Anne Brown
Patrick Doherty
Paula Renfroe

Brown's Chapel Elementary School
Tammy Anselmo
Brandi Breneman
Freda Mapes
Paige Mossman
Michele Slusher
Lorrie Spickard
Anna Sturm

Buchanan Elementary School
Rebecca Foster
Samantha Freeland
Heather Stuppy

Cedar Grove Elementary School
Stacey Harp
Kara Mullican

Central Office
Lisa Kegler

Central Middle School
Dulce Heim
Susan Mulraine
Lisa Murphy
Jennifer Paris

Christiana Elementary School
Brenda Adams
Amanda Amirault
Renay Anderson
Jeanie Barrett
Christy Brown
Leslie Cherry
Kathleen Davis
Nancy Duke
Lillie Erin Dwyer
Lynne Fox
Lynda Gupton
Deborah Henderson
Blake Hill
Cindy Keith
Melissa Mankin
Rebecca Miller
Teresa Miller
Elizabeth Minatra
Kathilu Mote
Tammy Noblin
Rachel Peters
Dawn Sweeney
Lacy Tallman
Jaime York
Sue Young

Christiana Middle School
Carol Haislip

Daniel McKee Alternative School
Patricia Smith

Eagleville School
Beverly Noland Barnes
Melissa Broyles
Theresa Hill
Bill Jarboe
Carla McElwee
Leslie Trail

Holloway High School
Jennifer Williams

Homer Pittard Campus School
Cindy Cliché
Kathy Paul

John Colemon Elementary School
Darlene McKinney

Kittrell Elementary School
Mary Merrill
Pam Todd
Kayla Weller
Ashley Whitaker

Lascassas Elementary School
Donna Cowan
Jennifer Frazier
Melissa Kincaid
Wanda Locker
Christina McAlexander
JoLyn McWhorter

LaVergne High School
Kay Trobaugh

LaVergne Middle School
Patricia Campbell
Tarron Huddleston
Jacquelyn McMeen
Katy Scala

LaVergne Primary School
Desiree Richards
Cindy Shively

McFadden School of Excellence
Debra Brown
Elena Burgess
Kathy Daugherty
Cindy Davis
Lark Petty
Vanessa Tipton

Oakland High School
Nancy Jackson

Riverdale High School
Ruth Taylor
Patrick White

Rock Springs Elementary School
Jill McHenry
Lisa Ransburgh

Rock Springs Middle School
Diana Barton
Deborah Hunt
Priscilla James

Rockvale Elementary School
Jennie Griffin
Mary Patterson
Amber Petricca

Roy Waldron Elementary School
Andrea Bontempi
Victoria Duff
Lori Foutch

Siegel High School
Kim Cing
Eileen Haynes
Belinda Juergens
Melissa LaDuc
Matt Marlatt
Trish Morgan
Sarah Smith
Barbara Zawislak

Siegel Middle School
Teri Beck
Sandra Boyd
Allison Brownlow
Sonya Cox
Edie Emery
Dolinda Huffman
Jason Manley
Susan Royston
Karla Steward

Smyrna Elementary School
Emily Beavers
Rebecca Dunn
Jason Eaton
Lynda Gupton
Kathy McMahan

Smyrna High School
Pamela Brown
Rachel Chitwood
Sarah Esberger
Jean Lemke
Michael Otto
Rachel Phillips
Kris Pollack
Jill Walls
Kelly Wester

Smyrna Primary School
Pamela Garner
Emily Lowery
Jennifer Monroe
Boe Washington

Smyrna West Alternative School
Kara Porter
Laura Schlesinger

Stewarts Creek Elementary School
Lynda Gupton

Stewarts Creek Middle School
Jane Macomber

Thurman Francis Arts Academy
Shanya Caldwell
Nancy Essary
Janelle Gehrke
Lynda Gupton
Diane McElroy
Sandra Muggu
Jane Mullins
Mary Ross
Hillary Stephens
Beth Tuverson

Walter Hill Elementary School
Teresa Brockwell
Beverly Carlton

Wilson Elementary School
René Davis
Valorie Estes
Amanda Henry
Jacqueline Hooper
Laurie Kincaid
Aimee Lovvorn
Kristen Lucas
Rachel Peay
Angela Steagall